FOLK CRAFTS FOR WORLD FRIENDSHIP

Haitian style metal fish,
see page 114.

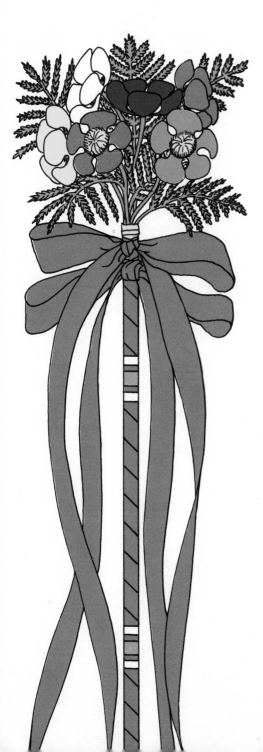

Folk Crafts for World Friendship

Florence Temko
Illustrated by Yaroslava

DOUBLEDAY & COMPANY, INC.,
GARDEN CITY, NEW YORK

Library of Congress Catalog Card Number 76–4215

ISBN 0-385-11115-0 Trade
0-385-12349-3 Paperbound

ILLUSTRATIONS ON PAGE 1:

Two belts from Guatemala in the Indian tradition
that has been handed down from generation to
generation for thousands of years. Belts not only hold
up pants and skirts, but the patterns may tell the
wearer's age or act as a talisman against evil.

For Stephen and Ellen

Other Books by Florence Temko:

PAPERFOLDING TO BEGIN WITH

PAPER CUTTING

FELT CRAFT

PAPER: FOLDED, CUT, SCULPTED

SELF-STICK CRAFTS

DECOUPAGE CRAFT

THE BIG FELT BURGER

CONTENTS

CELEBRATIONS

MASKS AND COSTUMES

TOYS

DECORATIONS

GAMES

ABOUT THE BOOK

This book is about traditional crafts in many countries. Each chapter is about a craft from one country and is divided into three parts:

1. The story about the craft.
2. Step-by-step directions for using this craft to make something.
3. Suggestions for "What Else You Can Do."

The third section of each chapter is intended to lead you to adapt the crafts to suit yourself, which may well be the most exciting of all.

I hope you will enjoy making the many different things and being part of the international craft tradition.

ABOUT MEASUREMENTS

Dimensions are given in inches followed by metric measurements in parentheses. As most people find it much easier to work with round figures I have used them whenever possible and avoided fractions. Therefore, the centimeter measurements may not always be quite accurate conversions.

You are invited to an international party. Open the pages of this book and meet the guests bearing gifts from all over the world: a wooden balancing toy from Pakistan, a numbers game from Africa, leather puppets from Greece, a woven vest from Colombia, a clay Menorah candleholder from Israel, an Eskimo string trick, and many more.

ABOUT CRAFTS

When primitive people needed cooking pots, they dug clay soil and shaped it into pottery; they gathered sheep's hair and pounded it into felt for clothing and blankets; they cut trees to build houses. Through the ages these simple crafts became more sophisticated. Each generation refined what had been done before, just as your drawing ability improves the more you draw. Pots were glazed with chemicals, producing lovely colors when baked in hot kilns. Intricate weaving patterns made clothes individual. Masks and costumes protected the wearer against evil and added color to festivals. The makers used all the natural materials found near where they lived, and every society developed its own patterns by which they were known.

With the invention of machinery, mass-produced merchandise began to replace handicrafts, but people missed the satisfaction of making things with their own hands. You may have experienced this yourself. Perhaps you made a puppet and after many tries you were pleased when you achieved just the right smiling face. Or you embroidered clothes to express your personality. Any little imperfections in this kind of handwork add a special charm.

World Friendship Tree

A world friendship tree is a Christmas tree that lasts all year and is decorated with a changing display of folk art and other things from all over the world. You can make it from branches sprayed white or from cardboard or wire. A friendship tree is a wonderful group project. At our house we hang on it any colorful piece of "found art," which may be decorated eggs, dried leaves, *origami*, an illustration of a child from another country, or anything unusual we don't know what to do with but is too nice to throw away. When we need space we take off something we have looked at long enough. At other times we decide to remove everything and start all over. Friends always want to see what's new, and they also bring things. Sometimes one of the children "owns" the tree and is in charge of decorating it.

To make a real friendship tree, exchange small gifts with a friend, or better still with someone from another city or another country. There are no rules. Start looking at everything to see whether it is suitable for your tree. You can highlight different countries and collect things from, say, Mexico. Next you can have a Scandinavian tree. Begin with a country from which you already own something or about which you know a lot. You can have a monthly festival tree. Beginning in January, decorate with wintry icicles made from kitchen foil. In February hang up hearts and valentine greetings. Follow it up with an Easter egg tree, using decorated plastic or blown eggs. And so on through the year. In July make paper dolls in honor of the Japanese Tanabata festival. October is the time for small jack-o'-lanterns and black witches, and soon after that it's time for a Christmas tree.

This "Fest" tree is lighted by the Danish Hamann family
whenever someone comes to their house for the first time.

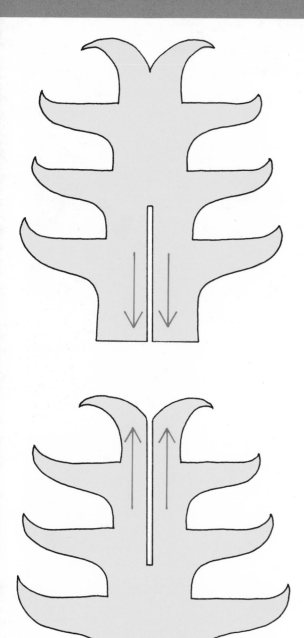

HOW TO MAKE
THE FRIENDSHIP TREE

Make the tree from two large pieces of corrugated cardboard. Cut them both into a tree with a wide trunk. Cut a slit in the center of both trees. One tree is slit halfway down from the top. The other tree is slit halfway up from the bottom. Slide the notched trees into each other.

You can make the tree from branches, stuck into a vase or a painted can.
Or cut several lengths of stiff wire. Stick the wires into a pot with plaster of Paris or pebbles. Curve the other to act as branches on which to hang things.
Make a tree from an old lamp or any other junked thing.

HOW TO HANG THINGS

With nylon thread or wool yarn.
With Christmas tree ornament hangers.
With masking tape shaped into loops.

WHAT TO HANG

Paper monsters

Miniature animals

Geometric solids

Cardboard triangles with cutouts from advertisements or colored paper

Shells, beads, sequins

Metal washers spray-painted gold

Yarn hanging in strands like icicles

Yarn dolls

Origami

Small empty bottles

Doll furniture

Anything handmade

Corrugated cardboard tree, painted white, 18″ (45 cm) high, 18″ (45 cm) wide. Decorated with folk craft and family souvenirs.

IDEAS FOR ONE-THEME TREES

Foreign festivals	Shapes: circles, hearts, triangles
Plants	Zodiac signs
Animals	Photos
Stamps	Religious decorations
Everything made from paper	One color only
Everything made from clay	Two colors

Sinterklaas Surprises

St. Nicholas, or Santa Claus, is the patron saint of children. He was a bishop who lived in Myra in Asia Minor in the fourth century and is reputed to have brought back to life some babies who had drowned in salt water. In Holland he is called Sinterklaas. On his name day—December 6—he has brought gifts to Dutch children for six hundred years, and it is the most exciting day of the year.

The story every Dutch child knows is that on December 5 he comes by ship from Spain. His arrival at a different Dutch port each year is televised. Afterward, he continues on to Amsterdam, where large crowds turn out to greet him in person as he rides on his white horse accompanied by his assistant, Zwarte Piet (Black Peter).

Before the holiday small children try to be very good as otherwise Zwarte Piet may smack them with a birch branch—or even worse, take them away in his big bag. Adults and older children are busy preparing surprise gifts for others in secret. They must be wrapped in unusual or funny ways with a tag written in verse attached. Then they have to be hidden in closets or under the bed.

On *Sinterklaas Avond* (evening), children place their shoes by the chimney, filling them with carrots, lumps of sugar, or hay for the white horse. They are hoping to find these tidbits replaced in the morning with gifts from Sinterklaas, but if they really misbehaved during the year, they will find a birch switch instead. In some homes children put out old-fashioned wooden clogs instead of their own shoes.

Before Sinterklaas and Piet ride across the roofs at night to distribute gifts, they visit every town and village. In some homes the doorbell rings and Piet's black-gloved hand throws in a lot of cookies and candies, quickly slamming the door shut again. The children scramble for the sweets and the mother looks outside to see what is going on. She acts surprised to find a big basket full of packages, which she pulls inside.

In most homes presents are not opened until the small children have finally gone to bed, dreaming about what they will find in their shoes in the morning. Then the rest of the family unwraps the surprises. The attached poems, all signed Sinterklaas, are read aloud, and as they are personal and funny, a lot of giggling and laughing goes on. Perhaps Mother receives a small kitchen gadget hidden in a huge box painted to look like a stove, with a poem about the many nice things she has done or kidding her about burning the vegetables.

Traditional sweets are marzipan, which is made from almond paste and shaped into fruit or soap or sausages or other funny things; and initials which are made from chocolate or almond pastry.

As you can see, a lot of jokes are associated with St. Nicholas Day, and the whole country is festive and merry. In contrast, Christmas is celebrated more quietly around the Christmas tree.

WHAT YOU CAN DO

Have a St. Nicholas party on December 5 or 6. Or exchange silly gifts for a birthday or class party. Set a limit on how much everyone can spend on a gift, but no limit on the tricky way in which it can be presented. A small package can be hidden inside a cored apple, with the core carefully replaced. Or wrap a tiny gift in foil or plastic and bury it in Jello. How about a treasure hunt? Write clue number 1 on a piece of paper, which you gift wrap. This leads to more clues all over the house and the last clue leads to the gift, which is taped under the table where everyone is sitting.

But don't forget, poems are essential. Here is a sample of what Hans may find on a package of warm gloves:

On a gift of buttons:

To Hans

Homework he hates
But he's fast on his skates.

Sinterklaas

She sews a straight seam,
A beautiful dress,
Her name is Jean,
Her room is a mess.

Sinterklaas

Another verse:

To Anna

She made it,
She made it,
What did she do?
She won the trophy for our school.

Sinterklaas

Not all *Sinterklaas* party poems are so short. In fact, they may have many verses and are often decorated with art work.

It's time to open Sinterklaas
gifts which are hidden
inside amusing packages.

First-Day-of-School Cone

Everyone remembers the first day of school. Most children can hardly wait for it, but are also a little afraid. To sweeten the day, children in Germany receive a large paper cone filled with candies and cookies from their parents. The cones can be bought in German stores or made at home from colored poster board and crepe paper. You can adapt this idea for Christmas, Valentine's Day, or other occasions. The cones are easy to make and, when filled, can be given as presents or exchanged at a school or Scout party.

HOW TO MAKE THE CONE

you need

Poster board or stiff paper
Crepe paper
A piece of ribbon
Sticky tape
White glue

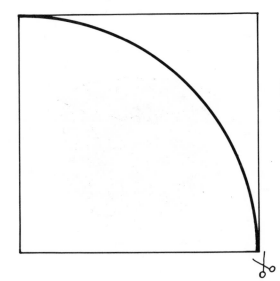

MAKING THE CONE

1. Cut paper 22″ (55 cm) square. Draw a curved line from one corner to the opposite corner. Cut out on that line.

2. Roll the poster board so that the two straight edges overlap several inches.

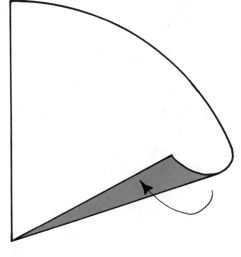

Little sister on her way on the first day of school with *Schultüte* filled with sweet things. The boy wears the typical German brief case on his back.

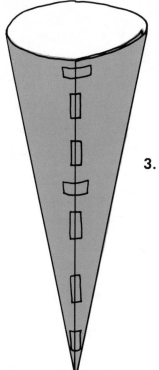

3. Hold them together with sticky tape.

MAKING THE TOP

4. Cut a piece of crepe paper 12″ (30 cm) wide and long enough to go around the top of the cone. Glue it inside the cone.

DECORATING THE CONE

In Germany paper decorations are usually glued on the cone. Make cut-outs from gift wrap. Glue gold-paper lace all around the top edge. Or cover the whole cone with gift-wrap paper.

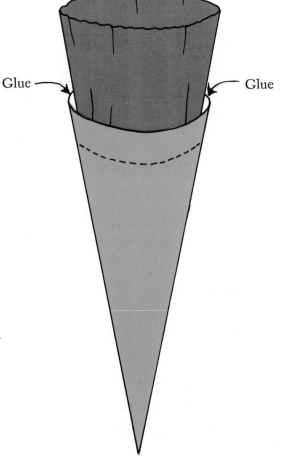

Glue — Glue

FINISHING

Fill the cone with cookies, candies, or small gifts and tie the top with ribbon.

WHAT ELSE YOU CAN DO

Make small paper cones for Christmas tree decorations.

Use paper cones as gift wraps. How about for a Sinterklaas surprise (see page 16).

Glue beads on the outside of the cone.

Make a candy-filled cone for your small brother or sister for the first day of school.

Tanabata Paper Decorations

Japan is a country of many colorful festivals, some dating far back into history. They may be religious or in honor of a local hero. If the word *matsuri* is part of the name, it indicates a Shinto festival. Shinto is the Japanese state religion, but people who observe Shinto rites may also practice Buddhism.

The greatest holiday is the New Year. Another important celebration is Boys' Day, when paper fish are flown on long poles. For the Doll Festival girls display beautiful sets of dolls dressed in imperial clothes. On Seven-Five-Three Day families visit a shrine to give thanks that their children have reached these ages and ask for future blessings. According to the Western calendar, the children are six, four, and two years old. But as every person in Japan becomes a year older on New Year's Day, a baby born on December 31 is automatically one year old the next day.

Towns and villages have their own local celebrations, and one could go to a festival in Japan on almost any day of the year. *Chagu-chaguumakko* is a rest day for work horses in the country district of Morioka. On *Kamakura* Day children in the snowy north of Japan build igloos, sitting snugly inside at a party in honor of the water god.

Groups of people travel together to attend festivals nearby or at faraway places, and each group is kept together by a guide waving a distinctive flag. Some women are dressed in kimonos, the national dress. Many travelers carry cameras as photography is the most popular hobby in Japan.

Tanabata Matsuri, the star festival, occurs on July 7, except in Sendai, where it is held a month later on August 6 through 8. Here the most famous and lavish decorations are displayed, and all the streets are festooned with huge streamers imitating the stars of the Milky Way. Bamboo branches decorated with paper dolls and prayer strips are placed in front of private homes. At the end of the holiday the branches are taken down and floated away on the river. All decorations are symbolic prayers for success in weaving, writing, and handicrafts.

Tanabata means weaving loom, and the festival commemorates the legend of Princess Shokujo and the shepherd boy Kenju who were stars in heaven. Princess Shokujo was weaving a piece of cloth to be made into a coat for her father, the heavenly king. During the many months required to finish it Princess Shokujo fell in love with Kengyu. They made plans to be married and spent every possible hour together. As a result Shokujo forgot to weave the cloth, which annoyed the king. He shouted, "You are not doing your work! I won't let you see Kengyu any more." In punishment he sent Shokujo to live at one end of the Milky Way and Kengyu at the other end, but permitted them to meet one day in the year. There was only one problem: There was no bridge over the Milky Way. How were they to meet even on that day? Fortunately, the birds loved Princess Shokujo and offered to make a bridge with their outspread wings.

HOW TO MAKE TANABATA DECORATIONS

you need

Paper squares, 6″ (15 cm) or other sizes

CHAINS

1. Fold square on lines as shown. UNFOLD. Turn paper over.

2. Fold on the diagonal. UNFOLD. Fold on the other diagonal.

Push   Push

3. Hold paper exactly as shown. Push it gently together until it forms a triangle.

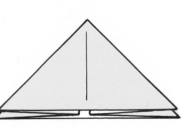

String many triangles together as shown in the photo of the *Tanabata festival*.

PAPER BALL

With some added folds, the triangle can be made into a ball.

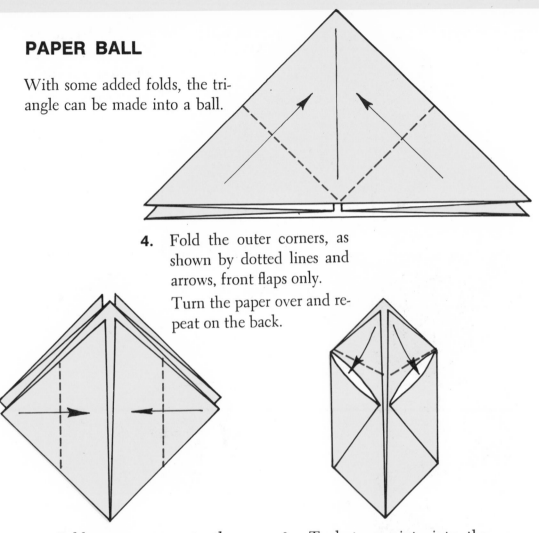

4. Fold the outer corners, as shown by dotted lines and arrows, front flaps only. Turn the paper over and repeat on the back.

5. Fold outer corners to the center. Turn paper over and repeat on the back.

6. Tuck top points into the two pockets shown, on the front and then on the back. They do not go in all the way. Turn paper over and repeat on the back.

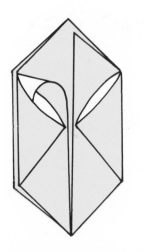

7. The ball is now ready to be inflated. Slide your forefinger behind the paper as shown. Put your thumb on the outside to hold the folds together. Put other hand on the other side in the same way. Blow into the little hole, at the same time moving your hands gently apart. After the ball is blown up it may need a little shaping to make it more even.

Balls can also be strung into tanabata chains.

Vary the sizes.

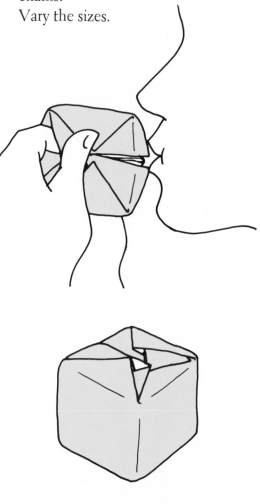

WHAT ELSE YOU CAN DO

Celebrate Tanabata in your class. Decorate the room with paper chains. Make up poems about crafts and hobbies, such as sewing, painting, stamp collecting, needlepoint, woodworking. Hold a handicraft exhibit, which is customary in Japan at the time of this festival.

Find out about Japanese writing and copy ideograms, which are pictures of words.

Find out the names of stars.

The ball is only one example of the art of paperfolding. This is a favorite hobby of Japanese children and is called *origami*. Make other things by folding paper squares and find more *origami* patterns in books.

Use the chains and balls for Christmas decorations or mobiles.

Tanabata Matsuri written in Japanese characters. Literally translated they mean Seventh Evening Festival.

Santa Lucia Crown

The Swedish Christmas season begins with Santa Lucia's Day, *Luciadagen*, on December 13. The oldest girl in the family represents Santa Lucia, the saint of light. She is dressed in white with a red sash and perhaps red tights. Her crown is made of lingonberry leaves and five lighted candles. Early in the morning she prepares a tray on which she puts a pot of coffee and yellow Lucia cat buns, *lussekatter*, so called because the raisins look like cats' eyes. In some families Santa Lucia alone brings the tray to her parents in their bedroom, or she may visit every sleeper in the house and wake them with a song and offer them coffee and a bun. In large families Santa Lucia may be accompanied by her sisters and cousins, all of them dressed in white, and they visit only the youngest girl. In any case, Santa Lucia must serve the buns herself, otherwise they will taste bitter and bring bad luck, but she may accept help with the coffeepot.

Throughout the day celebrations continue in schools, offices, and factories. Many towns hold contests to select a local girl to be Santa Lucia. It is much like a beauty contest, except that her kind personality is more important than her looks. She leads a parade seated on a float, with girl and boy attendants dressed in white. The boys wear high pointed hats decorated with golden stars. In Stockholm, Santa Lucia is crowned at the City Hall by the winner of the Nobel Prize for Literature.

You may wonder how this custom came about. December 13 is the name day of Santa Lucia who lived in Italy in the second century A.D. She believed strongly in the Christian religion, which was outlawed at the time. She wanted her family to give away all their money to poor people, but they did not like the idea at all!

One day her mother became ill and Lucia persuaded her to make a pilgrimage to a Christian holy place. Lucia's mother was cured and in gratitude for this miracle agreed to give away her wealth. Soon the government discovered that Lucia was a Christian and put her to death. Centuries later in honor of her good deeds she was declared a saint. Because the name Lucia means light, she became the saint of light and vision.

Although this story dates back hundreds of years, *Luciadagen* was observed in only a few Swedish villages until recently. There it was believed that Santa Lucia could be seen on her name day, when it is always cold, serving hot food and drink to poor people. The ceremony of serving coffee and buns may well recall this appearance.

In Sweden the winter nights are so long that on some days in the far north daylight lasts only an hour. Santa Lucia Day falls on one of the shortest days in the year, and what could be more cheerful than to honor her with this festival of light.

Saint Lucia Day celebrations are also held in some other countries, such as Switzerland. In San Diego, California, it is the custom for boats decorated with lights to tour the bay. Swedish families living in foreign countries continue to observe their native festival and begin the day with coffee and *lussekatter*.

HOW TO MAKE A SANTA LUCIA CROWN

In the olden days Santa Lucia crowns were made with pine branches and real candles. To keep the branches from catching fire, a damp cloth was placed between them. Nowadays ready-made crowns with batteries are sold in Sweden. You can make such a crown with Christmas bulbs and flashlight batteries, but it is easier just to roll up some paper into pretend candles.

you need

White drawing paper
Stapler, glue, and sticky tape
Orange-colored crayon

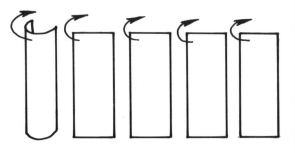

1. Cut 5 pieces of paper 2"×5" (5×12 cm). Roll each piece into a candle. (If the paper is stiff and difficult to roll, pull it over the edge of a table first.) Glue the two long edges together.

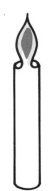

2. Cut one end to look like a candle flame and color it orange.

3. For the headband, cut a heavy piece of paper 25″ (60 cm) long and 1½″ (4 cm) wide.

4. Fasten the candles to the headband with sticky tape or staples. Cut a lot of leaves from green paper and attach them to the headband.

5. Fit the crown around your head and fasten it with staples or sticky tape.

FOR THE BOYS' HATS

you need

Large white drawing paper or poster board
Sticky tape

Cut paper 18″ (45 cm) square. Follow directions for making the paper cone on page 21. In taping the cone together, fit the size to your head.

STAR DECORATIONS

Trace the star shown on this page on a thin piece of paper and cut it out. Use it as a paper pattern for cutting out several five-pointed stars. Color them gold or cut them from gold paper. Then glue them to the hat.

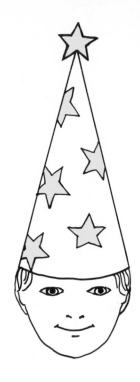

SANTA LUCIA BUNS

Ingredients: 2½ cups Bisquick
                ½ cup milk
                1 egg
                4 tablespoons cooking oil
                1 cup of flour

Mix and shape the dough into ½" (1 cm) thick rolls and cut them 5" long (12 cm). For each bun cross two strips into an X and curl the ends. Place a raisin in each of the curls. Bake at 375 degrees for 12 minutes.

Ice with 1 cup confectioners' sugar mixed with 3 teaspoons milk and a few drops yellow food coloring. Brush onto warm buns and dot with raisin eyes.

Santa Lucia buns are also made with 10" (25 cm) strips of dough curled into S shapes and decorated with raisins. The raisins always signify the cats' eyes.

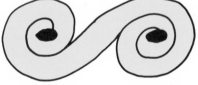

WHAT ELSE YOU CAN DO

Celebrate Santa Lucia Day in your class, at Scouts, or other meetings. Select Santa Lucia by writing every girl's name on a piece of paper and putting it into a box.

A blindfolded person picks out the name of the girl chosen to be Santa Lucia. She wears the crown and all the other girls wear tinsel headdresses and belts, while all the boys wear cone hats.

Perhaps somebody will volunteer to bake buns for the occasion. Otherwise serve cookies.

Finnish Christmas rolls are made with the same sweet dough, but shaped into boys and girls. The body, head, legs, and arms are made from separate pieces of dough and assembled directly on the cookie sheet. Eyes, mouth, and nose are made with raisins.

New Year's Paper Cut-Outs

New Year's is the most important Chinese holiday. It begins when the first moon appears, which may be in January or February. Huge dragons dance up and down the streets, and firecrackers explode everywhere as loud as gunfire. According to legend, New Year's was originally a celebration for conquering a monster.

Long, long ago a huge monster came out of the big Yellow River, which is yellow with mud and flows thousands of miles through China. The monster attacked people living on the river banks and damaged their houses and farms. It came year after year and the people tried to make it happy with offers of good food and expensive gifts. When that did not work, they built high stone walls to keep it away, but it climbed over the walls and ruined their villages again. Every kind of magic they tried was useless.

One day a wise old man said, "It seems to me that the monster is afraid of loud noises, bright lights, and the color red." Desperate and ready to

try anything, the villagers prepared for the time the monster was due to appear again. They painted their houses red, lighted all the lamps they owned, and banged their cooking pots loudly against each other. You never heard such a noise or saw so many lanterns swinging in the wind, throwing scary shadows. All night long the people kept up a frenzy . . . and the monster did not come. The monster was beaten, and to make sure it will not come back, Chinese people celebrate the New Year's holiday with dragon parades, noisy firecrackers, and paper lanterns carried high on sticks.

All members of a family are expected to travel from near and far to the home of the oldest male relative. They join in a big New Year's Eve dinner and nobody goes to bed that night. It would be unlucky. All New Year's customs are observed to ensure good fortune for the coming year. On New Year's Day everyone wears something new. Young people visit their grandmother and other relatives. Children receive red envelopes, with gifts of money, always in an even-numbered amount. A gift of three dollars is unlucky, unless it is presented in six half-dollar coins. A lot of cr-

The dragon dance is performed by two men with a papier-mâché mask, while drums, cymbals, and firecrackers make an unbearable noise to frighten away evil spirits.

Children with firecrackers about to go off.

anges are eaten during the visits. Their golden color denotes money, and the gift of an orange is a good wish for wealth.

The portrait of someone who died during the year is delivered at this time. In the days before photography an artist brought along a book showing various features. Relatives picked out the eyes, nose, and mouth which they thought resembled the deceased relative. When painting a living person, the artist was sometimes asked to include a secret message which could only be deciphered by the rightful heir.

All business debts are settled before New Year's. Merchants compete with each other in setting off the largest number of firecrackers, which are intended to chase away evil spirits. Gunpowder was invented by the Chinese many centuries ago to make loud noises and beautiful fireworks to imitate thunder and lightning.

Houses are cleaned before the holiday. Paper cutouts are popular interior decorations. Old ones are taken off the walls and windows at this time and replaced. Families make their own cutouts from red paper or, more often, buy them ready-made in the market. They look complicated, but handmade paper cutouts can be quite simple, and the instructions show how anyone can make them.

A Chinese girl with *Lai She*, or lucky money packets, an orange tree, greeting cards, and a New Year's toy.

Street celebration.

Rooster cutout made from red tissue paper. Instructions show how you can make it.

LEFT: New Year's visit to pay respects to grandmother.

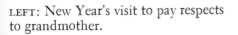

HOW TO MAKE PAPER CUTOUTS

you need

Thin colored paper
Small pointed scissors

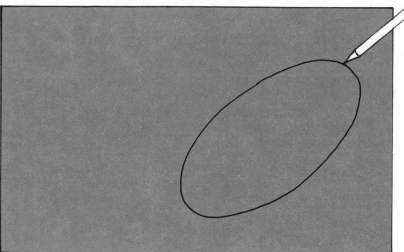

CHINESE ROOSTER

1. First *draw* the oval body.

2. Add an oval for the tail.

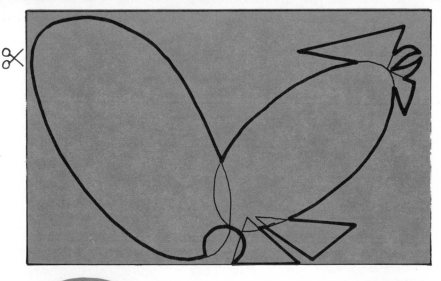

3. Draw triangles for the feet, comb, and beak. Draw a heavy line around the edges and *cut* on this outline.

4. Cut feathers into the tail, claws into the feet, then cut the eye and comb.

For practice cut out a few more roosters. Try cutting them without drawing the outline first.

WHAT ELSE YOU CAN DO

The Chinese calendar is grouped into a twelve-year cycle and each year is named after an animal sign of the oriental zodiac. The twelve creatures are:

The Rat	The Dragon	The Monkey
The Ox	The Snake	The Rooster
The Tiger	The Horse	The Dog
The Hare	The Sheep	The Boar

Try to make cutouts for all twelve animals. Build them up from parts, as you did for the rooster, or cut them in your own way. Paste the signs in a circle for a complete horoscope.

Paper cutouts made by Chinese folk artists. The styles vary from region to region.

In Chinese books cutouts are often used as illustrations. You can use them for greeting cards by pasting them on folded construction paper or thin cardboard.

This dragon carried in a Chinese New Year's parade is cut by an expert paper cutter. Note the connecting "bridges" that hold the parts of the design together. The eyes and the nose are connected to the face. Each person is joined to the next one.

Wedding Dance Pole

The Hungarian word *lakodalom* means both "wedding" and "feast," which gives you the idea that the most important celebration in Hungary is a wedding. As everywhere else in the world there is a lot of good eating and drinking, but in Hungary the dances and jokes are really boisterous.

Country weddings are celebrated with customs dating back to the time when brides were bought or kidnapped, even though their families tried to protect them. Symbolically, barriers are still placed in the path of a wedding procession to show that the bride is precious and not given up easily.

In many parts of the country the guests dress in national costume with a great deal of embroidery. Women wear layers of petticoats under their skirts, which are made of expensive fabrics as a status symbol.

The old customs are best preserved in remote mountain areas, and relatives come from far away to the feast, which may last several days. In some traditional dances the bridegroom and his friends twirl colorful sticks which are fancy versions of shepherds' staffs. They are decorated with fresh flowers as a sign of male strength and with ribbons in the national Hungarian colors of red, white, and green.

The bride in her wedding costume.

ON THE OPPOSITE PAGE: The best man toasting the wedding couple.

The groom holds up the wedding dance pole.

HOW TO MAKE THE POLE

you need

A dowel stick, about 5″ (12 mm) thick
6 yards (6 m) red ribbon
¼ yard (25 cm) white ribbon
¼ yard (25 cm) green ribbon
Flowers—fresh or plastic
White glue and sticky tape

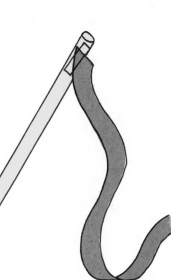

1. Cover the stick with red ribbon. Attach the ribbon at an angle to the end of the dowel with sticky tape.

2. Twirl the dowel, and the ribbon will wind around it. Put a dab of glue every few inches. Never mind a few wrinkles.

3. In the two places shown, glue on pieces of white and green ribbon.

4. Attach flowers to the top of the stick with sticky tape.

5. Cut a piece of red ribbon 2 yards long. Tie it in a bow around the stick and let the long ends of the ribbon hang down. Tie another bow exactly like it just below.

WHAT ELSE YOU CAN DO

Make ribbon poles as a good-luck decoration for someone's wedding.

Make the pole when you study about Eastern European countries.

Use it as a decoration for any party.

Make miniature poles as gift-wrap decoration. Stick one or more on the corners of the box.

Carry the poles as props in a play or a dance performance.

Instead of ribbon use paper cut into 1″ (2 cm) wide strips.

Decorate dowel sticks in your own fantasy way.

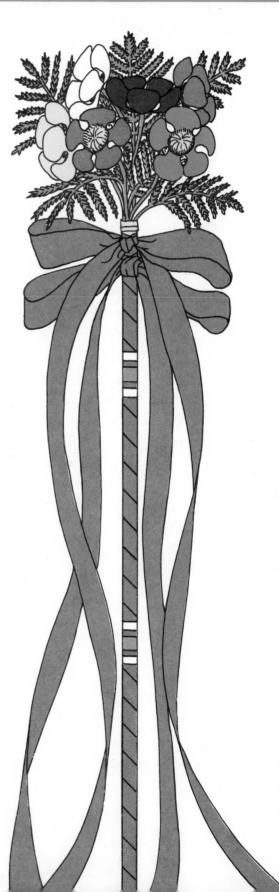

Posada Clay Figures

Feliz Navidad—Merry Christmas—in Mexico is a party every evening from December 16 to 24. And every evening children receive gifts of candy and small toys.

This is what happens: Nine familes celebrate together, and a *Posada* party is held at each family's house in turn. The word *posada* is Spanish for inn, and every party begins with a procession acting out Joseph and Mary's journey from Nazareth to Bethlehem, which took nine days. Two children lead the parade from room to room in the house or from door to door outdoors. They carry a tray with clay figures of Joseph and Mary, and the others follow carrying lighted candles. They represent the angel and the holy pilgrims. They knock at every door in the house, asking, "Is there room at the inn?" The innkeeper replies, "No, there is no room at the inn," and the journey continues until the procession reaches the last door, where the innkeeper permits them to enter. The room represents the stable where the Christ Child was born and here is set up the *nacimiento* or crèche of the Nativity. Angels, doves, and animals show up in the soft candlelight. The figures of Mary and Joseph are placed in the crèche on eight nights. Only on the ninth night, *La Noche Buena* (Christmas Eve), the figure of baby Jesus is carried in the procession and completes the scene.

You may imagine how it feels to be at a *Posada* party if you remember the excitement you feel at any big celebration; add the sound of hymns in your ears as the candle procession moves along. But this is only the beginning. The *piñata* game is the main attraction. A *piñata* may look like an animal, a bird, or a star and is strung between two walls of a courtyard. A few days before, the youngest child in the family chose it at the local market where thousands of *piñatas* are for sale at that time of the year. Vendors make them right in the street. They cover clay pots, such as you may use for plants, with strips of tissue paper until the pot is completely disguised. Donkeys and stars can be found every year, but the craftspeople also make new *piñata* designs.

For the *piñata* game everyone is blindfolded in turn and swings a big stick in an effort to break the *piñata*, which is filled with candy and small gifts. Everybody has a good time watching one of the boys whack the air nowhere near the *piñata*. Then his oldest sister, who is tallest, almost breaks it on her third try. But the rope that holds it is quickly pulled up. Everybody laughs and shouts happily that the *piñata* is saved and the game is not yet over. When the *piñata* finally breaks, all the goodies tumble out and children and adults alike all scramble for their share.

The ninth *Posada* party on Christmas Eve is celebrated with fireworks and lasts until midnight, when the whole family goes to hear Mass at the church. Christmas Day is a time for visiting and enjoying a specially good dinner. But the Christmas season is not yet over. The night before the Feast of Epiphany children put their shoes at the foot of their beds. During the night the Three Wise Men pass by on their way to see the Christ Child and leave the most wonderful gifts of all. After that the *nacimiento* is taken down and packed up until next Christmas.

Traditional Mexican crafts are best preserved in the Puebla Mountains, about a hundred miles south of Mexico City. The potters of the village of Metepec produce some of the most beautiful crèche figures which are sold before Christmas on market days all over Mexico.

HOW TO MAKE POSADA CLAY FIGURES

you need

Self-hardening or other clay
Small bowl with water
Ice-cream stick
Toothpick
Newspaper to work on

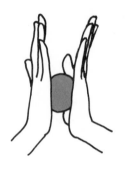

BASIC SHAPES

A ball: roll some clay around between the palms of both hands.

A sausage (cylinder): on a table top covered with newspaper, roll the clay with one hand.

COMBINING SHAPES

With the two basic shapes you can make any figure.

Always glue shapes together with water. Dip your finger in water and apply it to the areas to be joined. Then press the parts together. WITHOUT WATER THE FIGURES WILL FALL APART WHEN THEY ARE DRY.

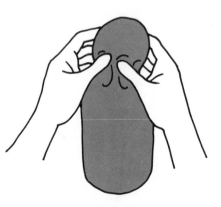

A VILLAGE WOMAN

1. For the body, take a lump of clay the size of a small apple; roll it into a short, fat sausage. Set it down flat.

2. For the head, make a ball the size of a large grape. Glue it to the body, smoothing the neck with your wet finger.

3. For the arms, make two small sausages and glue them on the body with water.

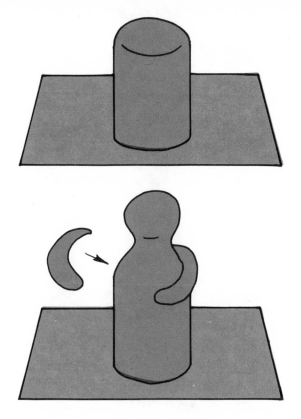

4. Smooth any rough parts on the figure with your wet finger.

5. The woman shown is carrying a bowl of fruit. The bowl is made from a small ball which is dented with the end of a pencil. The fruit is made from tiny balls of clay. The other crib figures are made in a similar way:

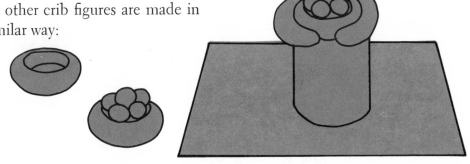

JOSEPH

1. Body is made from a lump of clay the size of an egg.
2. Head is made from a ball the size of a large grape and squeezed at one end for the beard.
3. The shepherd's staff is made from a sausage.
4. The arms are sausages.

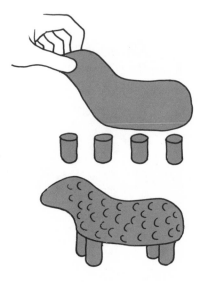

MARY

1. The body is made from a ball the size of a large plum.
2. The head is made from a ball the size of a large grape.
3. The legs are made from sausages. The feet are small balls which are squeezed to the legs and shaped a little.
4. The arms are two sausages pushed together in prayer.

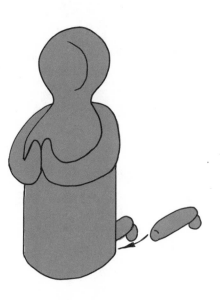

LAMB

1. Make a thick sausage and bend one end for the head. Squeeze it flat.
2. The legs are made from four short sausages.
3. Curly hair is indented with an ice-cream stick, or glue on pieces of cotton.

MORE FIGURES

The rest of the crib figures are made in the same way. As you begin each figure, measure the lump of clay by eye to make sure it will look well with the other figures. Mary should be a little smaller than Joseph. They can both be standing or kneeling. The manger is made from an egg-size ball of clay and pressed in with the thumb and shaped. Most crèches include a donkey.

DRYING AND BAKING

Let figures made from self-hardening clay dry for two days without touching them. Bake figures made from other clay according to directions on the package.
Paint the figures with tempera or acrylic paints.

HELPFUL HINTS

If any figure breaks after it is dry, glue it together with white glue (Elmer's, Sobo, or other).

If you don't like one of the things you have made from self-hardening clay, you can moisten it and use the clay over again.

Roll clay into a slab with a rolling pin or a straight sided mug. Then cut out shapes with a knife, cookie cutter, jar lid, the end of a straw or other utensils.

If you enjoy working with clay, find out about making pottery from a potter who lives in your area. You can usually find a craftsperson by asking an art teacher or at the local art store.

WHAT ELSE YOU CAN DO

Add more people and animals to your crèche. Mexican families accumulate new figurines each year to add to their *nacimiento*.

Build a landscape around the crèche. *Nacimientos* often have mountains made with green moss and roads made from sand. Many other details are added.

Illustrate fairy tales, Bible stories, or folk tales from foreign countries with clay figures.

Make figures into Christmas ornaments to hang on the tree. Push a paper clip into the figure before drying. Let the end of the clip peek out to be the hanger.

In Provence, France, Christmas crèche figures are dressed in the clothes representing their occupation: the baker, the postman, the grocery clerk, the mayor, all bearing gifts for the Christ Child. You can adapt this idea by making figures in present-day clothing or by looking in a book of costumes.

Hanukkah Candleholder

Hanukkah is the Jewish Feast of Light, which commemorates a battle won by the Jews in 165 B.C., as recorded in the Book of Maccabees. Two thousand years ago Antiochus, a Syrian king, governed Israel. He was determined that the Jews give up their belief in one God and take on the Greek religion instead. The Jews struggled to keep their own traditions. When their sacred temple in Jerusalem was overrun by the Syrian army, the Maccabee brothers formed a band to fight them.

In time other men joined them and after three years succeeded in driving away the soldiers. Their first thought was to relight the holy candelabra in the ransacked temple, but according to legend they could only find a tiny bit of sacred oil.

It was not even enough to last for one day, but to their surprise the light continued to burn for eight days. In memory of this miracle Jewish families celebrate Hanukkah every year for eight days by lighting a candlestick, called a Menorah, and saying prayers of thanks. As soon as the sun sets on the first evening one candle is lit; on the second evening two candles are lit, and so on. It is the custom to light the candles with an extra candle, which is called the *shammas*, the Hebrew word for servant. The *shammas* is lighted first with a match and then picked up to kindle the daily candles.

On the eighth night the Menorah is fully lighted with all eight candles and the *shammas* aglow. In Israel, during the time of Hanukkah, electric Menorahs appear in public buildings and shop windows for the enjoyment of people walking by, in the same way as lighted trees are displayed at Christmastime in other countries.

Hanukkah is the time of gift-giving, and Jewish children receive a present on every one of the eight nights. Sometimes it is Hanukkah *gelt*, money which they can spend or save. Other customs connected with this happy holiday are traditional songs and the game of *dreidl* or spinning top. A *dreidl* has four sides, each with a number on it. Everyone takes a turn at spinning it and counts the number of points that show on top when the *dreidl* lands. And, of course, there is always good food, including crispy potato pancakes, called *latkes*.

You may wonder why one year Hanukkah is celebrated on December 25, the same time as Christmas, but another year the candles are lighted at the beginning of December. The Jewish people use not only the standard calendar, which is based on the movement of the sun, but also their

An Israeli family celebrating Hanukkah.

own calendar, which is based on the movement of the moon. The moon calendar goes back more than 5,000 years. The year 1980 is 5741 according to the Jewish calendar.

The most important Jewish holidays are New Year, followed ten days later by the Day of Atonement, called Yom Kippur. These sacred religious days occur in September. Children enjoy Hanukkah more because it comes at the time when most of their schoolmates in Western countries celebrate Christmas. They do not feel left out when they go home to their own festival of light.

The instructions show how to make a Menorah from self-hardening or other clay. Forty-four candles are needed for a full eight-day celebration. You can use birthday candles or buy Menorah candles at Jewish temples.

A *dreidl* (spinning top) showing Hebrew letter that indicates the amount the player wins.

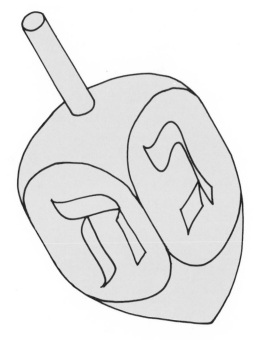

A MENORAH CANDLESTICK

you need

½ pound of self-hardening or other clay
Newspaper to work on
A piece of paper to make a pattern

MIXING THE CLAY

1. A *few hours before you want to use it,* mix the clay, following the instructions on the box.

PAPER PATTERN

2. On a thin piece of paper trace the triangle shown on this page. Then cut it out. Cut two more triangles exactly like it. Staple or glue them together to look like the drawing.

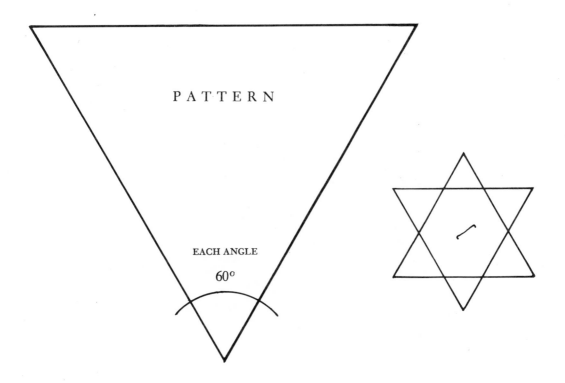

PATTERN

EACH ANGLE

60°

MAKING THE CANDLESTICK

3. Roll a blob of clay on a flat surface until it is about ½″ (1 cm) thick and 5″ (12 cm) long. Place it on one of the edges of your paper pattern.

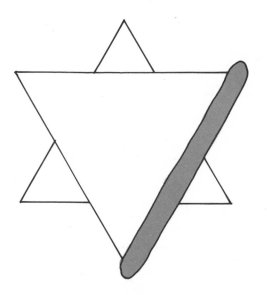

4. Make five more rolls like that and place them on the pattern.

5. Now glue the Menorah together. Put a little water in a cup. Dip your finger in the water and use it as glue wherever you want two parts to stay together. Round off the six corners in this way and press down where the rolls cross.

6. For the candleholders, roll eight little balls between the palms of your hands, each about ¾″ (2 cm) round. Make one larger ball, about 1″ (3 cm) round. Push the flat end of a pencil or ball-point pen into each ball, all the way through.

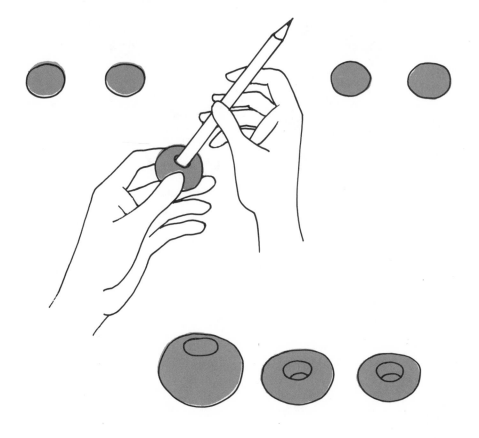

7. Glue the six candleholders to the corners with water. Glue two candleholders to the two intersections as shown. Glue on the large candleholder, as shown.

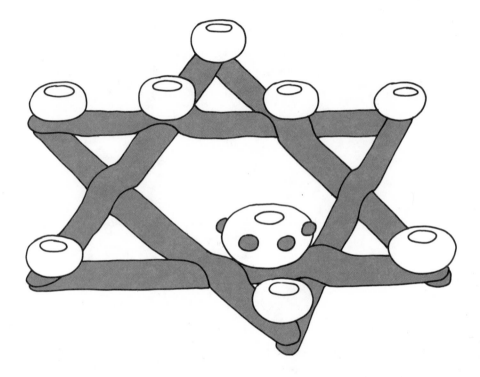

FINISHING

8. Dip your fingers in water and smooth out the parts with your fingers.

9. Add decorations as you please. Small clay beads have been added to the Menorah shown in the picture, but you can add all kinds of rolls and shapes, beads and sequins; or indent your initials or Hebrew letters with the point of a pencil.

10. Let the Menorah dry. *Do not touch it* for about two days. If clay needs to be baked, follow directions on the package.

PAINTING

11. When the Menorah is completely dry, paint it with tempera or acrylic paint. Blue and white are the national Israeli colors.

The Menorah is now ready for the celebration of Hanukkah. Do not push the candles in too hard, as the clay might break. If this should happen, glue it together with white glue.

WHAT ELSE YOU CAN DO

Cut out Hanukkah paper decorations: Menorahs, *dreidls*, Jewish flags, and stars.

Find out about other Jewish holidays and craft activities.

Find out about different calendars: Gregorian, Julian, Jewish, Aztec, Chinese, Hindu.

Another style Menorah which you can make with self-hardening clay.

Diwali Festival Lamp

The most important holiday in India is Diwali, in honor of Lakshmi who is the goddess of wealth and bliss, wife of the god Vishnu.

The *Diwali* festival of light is celebrated in October or November depending on the Hindu calendar. As the *deva* (goddess) Lakshmi has the power to bring wealth, it is the custom to pay all debts before the holiday so as to ensure her favor for the next year. Girls are busy making *dipa* lights which will be lit in front of a home altar displaying a picture of Lakshmi. They fill small earthenware bowls with oil and place wicks in them.

For the holiday the whole family dresses in their best clothes and family jewels in time for morning prayers. Breakfast is an elaborate meal, and even poor families try to serve some special dishes. Food varies from one part of the country to another. Although meat is not part of the diet, the vegetarian dishes are very tasty and highly spiced—most Indians find Western food too mild when they travel. The festive meal is served in small bowls placed on a round tray called *thali*. The center is filled with rice or a flat kind of bread called *chappaty*. Most Indians are accustomed to eating with their fingers and have developed certain rules that are con-

sidered polite. An Indian always uses the right hand for eating, and the food never reaches above the first joints of the thumb and two fingers.

The *Diwali* breakfast is followed by the children's favorite part of the day, the shooting of firecrackers. The streets are crowded as people watch Lakshmi's image being carried in procession. Bands are playing and paper streamers wave in the breeze. Stalls have sprung up everywhere, selling ice cream and sugar candy in the shape of the mythical monkey prince and other figures. Painted clay and paper toys are for sale: houses, towers, boats, men, elephants, horses, oxen, fish, and birds. Some of them have mechanisms to make them jump or perform other tricks.

As darkness falls, thousands of lamps are lighted on the edges of the roofs of buildings, to attract the blessing of Lakshmi. Some of the lights glow in red, green, or blue, turning the town into a twinkling fairyland. Glass flasks with colored water are placed in front of the *dipas* to produce the bright colors.

Later in the evening girls float lights across the river. If they reach the other shore still alight, the girl's family is assured of good fortune for the next year.

HOW TO MAKE A DIWALI LAMP

you need

Self-hardening, or other clay
A wick (for sale in candle shops, or use
   a piece of cotton string)
Salad oil

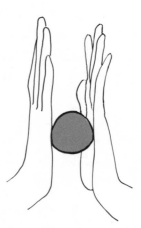

1. Roll a ball of clay, about
    2″ (5 cm).

2. Shape it into a bowl by
    pressing your thumb
    into the middle.

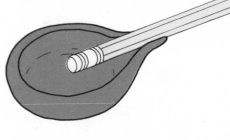

3. Make the wick holder by
    pulling the clay into a
    lip. Press a pencil into
    the lip. Let dry.

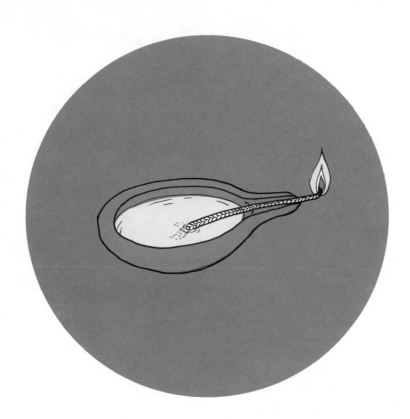

4. Put wick and oil in the bowl and light the lamp.

WHAT ELSE YOU CAN DO

Have a *Diwali* festival. Make an altar, with *dipas*, clay figures and other toys to honor Lakshmi.

Instead of clay lamps, use candles in a saucer, which is also done in India.

Put on a play: make scenery showing buildings with colored lights on the roofs and re-enact the customs related at the beginning of this chapter.

An Egyptian god from Trinidad. Just before Lent carnival is lavishly celebrated all over South America. Trinidad costumes are famous and many are engineering works of art fitted with electric lights. Although planned in advance, they develop in the making. Preparations for the festival take almost a year. Huge parades are accompanied by band competitions. Visitors come from all over the world to watch the spectacle.

Masks

Masks are magic disguises that can turn a person into an animal, a sorcerer, or whatever you please. Throughout the ages masks have been used for many different reasons.

Originally some masks were real animal heads. They transmitted the strength and power of that animal to the wearer, who was no longer a human being pretending to be a deer, but actually a deer who could run faster than the enemy.

Kachina masks are worn by Hopi Indians to impersonate kindly supernatural ancestors at ceremonies held to pray for rain and a good crop. The masks are made of rawhide which is shaped into a cylinder or other forms, and may be fitted with feathers, horns, and other natural ornaments.

South American tribal masks mostly accompany dances that are performed at a feast. This may be held for a harvest thanksgiving or at a funeral to chase away the evil spirits who caused the death.

African masks may accompany initiation rites when teen-age boys and girls are accepted as full adults.

Nowadays masks have different purposes. The doctor covers his face with surgical gauze to protect the patient against germs. The ice hockey goalkeeper protects his face against injury with a mask that looks quite ghoulish. But mostly masks are used for fun, to pretend you are somebody else for a while.

Huge masks create an eerie scene
in the opera *Tremonisha.*

HOW TO MAKE MASKS

The illustrations show masks from all over the world. Suggestions are given how you can imitate them, but they are really intended just to start you off on inventing your own. Different kinds of paper are the easiest materials to use, and any lightweight object can be attached as a decoration. Masks can be worn or hung on walls. Make them huge; make them tiny. Make them scary; make them grinning.

To wear masks, make two holes at the sides and tie on a piece of elastic or string.

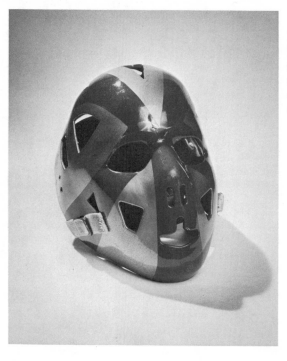

Ice hockey goalkeeper's mask made by Robert Lohbauer. He made a plaster of Paris mold of the player's face and covered it with Fiberglas. The player wanted green and gold stripes, which were painted with epoxy paint.

Helmet mask from Zaire. Wood and fiber, 17″ (42 cm) high. This mask is used in the circumcision ritual of the Hemba tribe. The antelope on top of the head symbolizes speed and dancing agility. The mask can be imitated with papier-mâché and raffia. More simply, a paper plate can be used for the face and paper strips added. The antelope can be made from clay.

Papier-mâché Devil mask from Venezuela. It could also be made from a paper plate, painted with tempera or acrylic.

Traditional Chinese theater mask with *yin-yang* symbols on the forehead. Use plaster of Paris or Pariscraft (gauze strips impregnated with plaster of Paris which harden after they are wet). Either material can be molded over a round bowl.

BELOW: Carved wooden mask from Japan. It is painted red and the hair is made of sisal. Farmers hang it near their rice fields to protect the harvest from evil spirits.

RIGHT: Elephant mask from the Ivory Coast. It is approximately 3' (1 m) long and made from a large palm leaf. This mask can be copied very well with Hypro paper sculpture fabric, available in art supply stores. Cut out the mask, dampen the paper, and form it. When dry, paint it with bright tempera or acrylic paint.

Halloween Costumes

Ghosts and witches, fairies and clowns, Martians and monsters roam the night at Halloween. They are costumed youngsters who knock at neighbors' doors and shout, "Trick or treat." The householders are prepared for the call of the spooky visitors with a supply of sweets, apples, and small coins, as well as triangular orange-colored sugar candy called candy corn or chicken feed. In recent years instead of asking for treats for themselves, many youngsters in the United States and Canada collect money for the United Nation's Children's Fund (UNICEF) to help needy children all over the world.

"Trick or treat" was started in America by Irish immigrants who continued to celebrate the festival of Samain as they had done in Ireland. On the evening of October 31 country lads went from house to house collecting food or money for a community celebration, sometimes around a bonfire. Farmers who gave freely were blessed, while stingy people were threatened with mischief.

Dressing up in costume dates back to the Druids in ancient England and Ireland, who believed that the spirits of the dead returned to haunt the living. People tried to chase them away by disguising themselves to fool the spirits into thinking they were one of them. The word Halloween is an abbreviation of All Hallows' Eve or the evening of All Souls' or All Saints' Day. This Roman Catholic holiday supplanted the pagan rituals, and the costumes then represented saints.

Remembrances of the dead are widely observed in many parts of the world. In Mexico, *el Dia de los Muertos* (Day of the Dead) on November 2, is not sad, but full of fun.

Markets sell all kinds of decorations and toys, many showing skeletons having a good time eating, drinking, playing guitars, and even riding bicycles. Bakeries sell bread in the shape of skulls. Mock funerals are held with hearses made of candy and corpses popping out of coffins. Many families spend the night at the cemetery, which is illuminated with bright yellow candles. They bring gifts of food to their dead relatives and sometimes sing and dance.

Because Halloween is observed to honor departed souls, ghosts and skeletons are popular costumes. But most people do not even remember this origin, and it is fun to dress up in any disguise.

It is always hard to decide what to wear, and first we think of the standard gypsy, pirate, king, or queen. But what is a costume? It is really anything that is not everyday clothing where we live. Regular clothing from one country looks like a costume somewhere else. A silk sari worn in India

Kläuse, masked figures, parade through the Swiss village of Urnäsch on January 13, which is New Year's Eve according to the old Julian calendar. Their headdresses are masterpieces of jigsaw work with intricate decorations. The *Kläuse* wear bells of all sizes, which jingle rhythmically as they stomp and dance. Local residents give them coins and other presents.

is unusual on a street in France; and Western ranchers wear cowboy boots every day. You can become a person from another country or a different century, but the costume does not have to be authentic to the last detail. Think of ways that are not usually considered costuming. Be an animal by cutting out a poster picture of a lion, glue it on cardboard and wear it. Be a growing plant by wearing a sheet dyed green and raising your arms slowly. Be a house by walking around in a large cardboard box, cut out windows you can see through, draw on doors and the roof. Look at pictures in books, magazines, and on television. Try to turn what you see into costumes. The more fantastic the better. If someone asks you, "And what is your costume?" you can reply, "It's a fantasy," or "I'm a being from another world." In this way you can experiment and make anything you like.

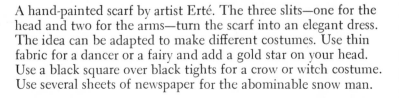

A hand-painted scarf by artist Erté. The three slits—one for the head and two for the arms—turn the scarf into an elegant dress. The idea can be adapted to make different costumes. Use thin fabric for a dancer or a fairy and add a gold star on your head. Use a black square over black tights for a crow or witch costume. Use several sheets of newspaper for the abominable snow man.

HOW TO MAKE COSTUMES

Halloween costumes are made to be worn only once.and should not take hours to make. Think of easy-to-make outfits as coming in parts:

1. BASIC COVERINGS. Wear plain colored jeans, leotards, tights, and shirt tops.

2. ONE-PIECE COVER-UPS. The simplest wrap-arounds are made from one piece of fabric, like sarongs, Roman togas, or modern wrap-around skirts; American Indian blankets and South American ponchos used as coats. They can be held in place by tucking in one corner (like a sarong) or with belts, string, safety pins, or buttons. A wrap-around costume can be a tramp huddled in a blanket or the elegant scarf dress by Erte shown here.

3. TWO-PIECE COVER-UPS. A little more elaborate clothing can be made from two pieces of cloth sewn together, one piece for the front of the body and another for the back. They can be cut to hip length for a male or female blouse, knee length, or down to the floor.

4. DECORATIONS. The cover-up can be painted or embroidered to indicate the specific costume you want. A Russian cossack costume can be made from a belted blouse worn with tights and high boots; paint on some flowers. Baste strips of kitchen foil to a cover-up to represent an electrical storm.

MATERIALS

For cover-ups, use old sheets and fabric remnants (sew or glue small pieces together), plastic sheeting, paper bags, double layers of newspapers or crepe paper (can be sewn if necessary).

For headdresses use remnants of fabric, scarves, bandanna, or dish towels. They convert easily into turbans.

Trimmings can be made with crayons, paint, felt-tip pens, buttons, shells (often used in Africa and Pacific islands), broken pieces of plastic, small empty plastic containers, aluminum kitchen foil for futuristic costumes, bits of furry fabrics, sewing accessories such as rickrack and bindings, ribbons, paper cutouts, doilies, self-stick plastic sheeting (Con-Tact®, etc.), bits of felt.

FASTENINGS

Glue, staples, buttons, needle and thread, sticky tape.

Pollera costume from Panama. It is made from a separate blouse and skirt and can be copied by gathering straight pieces of fabric on elastic. Paint the flowers with ball-point embroidery paint sold in dime and craft stores.

Cone-shaped costumes are found in various parts of the world. A New Guinea medicine man wears a costume made from straw with two large masks, one on top of the other. To make this costume, roll brown wrapping paper into a cone (see page 21). If necessary glue several sheets together to make a large sheet. Make two large paper masks and attach them to the cone.

Competing group in Trinidad carnival.

Pearlies

In London on weekends and holidays you may be surprised to see a few people dressed in clothes covered entirely with pearl buttons. Everywhere they go they are treated as though they were royalty. In fact, they are the Pearly King and Queen, and their children are Princes and Princesses.

The custom of decorating clothes with buttons was started around 1900 by the "Flashboys," who sold fruit and other goods from wagons in the street. To attract customers they sewed a line of buttons up the side of their trousers. Soon the decorations became more and more elaborate, as the Flashboys tried to outdo each other. Some covered every inch of their clothing with buttons, and others sewed them on in patterns. An official competition was held to select the man and woman with the flashiest costume and, they were crowned Pearly King and Queen at a festive ball. The title became hereditary and passed on to their children. Now there are few Pearlies left, and they are the center of attention wherever they go.

London's Pearly Kings and Queens
on parade.

WHAT YOU CAN DO

In a way, decorating jeans and tops with embroidery and paint is similar to pearly costuming. You can revive the fashion by sewing buttons on your clothes, inspired by the different patterns you see in the illustration.

Buttons, shells and a
chevron decorate a
prize-winning jacket in a
denim art contest.

Senufo mud painting: 40"×27" (100×68 cm). The fabric is
made of six woven strips, approximately 4½" (11 cm) wide, that
are sewn together.

Fabric Painting with Mud

The Senufo tribe on the Ivory Coast uses black slushy mud to paint fabrics. They have discovered just where to dig in nearby swamps for the right kind that produces a deep black dye that is long-lasting.

The fabric is stretched tightly and nailed to a wooden board. The outline of crocodiles, turtles, birds, fish and other animals is drawn with a thin dye made from boiled leaves. When this is dry the areas are filled in with the heavy mud paint with a toothbrush. Although the artists do not sign their names, it is often possible to distinguish one painter from another by a difference in style.

When completed, hunters wear the fabric as clothing, for a kind of camouflage. The black-and-white pattern is difficult to see among the trees and heavy undergrowth. The animal figures are symbolic protection against danger and are believed to help the hunter bring in a large catch.

HOW TO DO FABRIC PAINTING

The instructions show how you can paint fabric in the Senufo way with felt-tip pens. Be sure to get the *permanent* kind that is waterproof. You can use the painted fabric for a wall hanging or for clothing. If you decide to make a vest or skirt, first cut out the material according to the pattern; then paint it and sew it up.

you need

Unbleached muslin
Black felt-tip pen, permanent type

1. Cover your worktable with newspaper.

2. Draw animal and other designs on the muslin.
Before you start, think about what you want to paint. You may even want to make a rough sketch on paper first.

WHAT ELSE YOU CAN DO

Use *colored* felt-tip pens, permanent type.
Make greeting cards by pasting small painted
fabric pictures on construction paper.
Decorate jeans and shirts.
Make mud paintings on paper instead of fabric.
Make place mats.

Weaving

In Ghana, on the coast of West Africa, you can tell just by looking at a piece of cloth whether it was woven by a man or a woman. If the cloth is made up of strips 4 to 6 inches (10 to 15 cm) wide, it was made by a man. If the strips are 16 to 20 inches (40 to 50 cm) wide, it was made by a woman. This tradition developed because a man exchanges his weaving for food which his family needs. He travels from village to village, and it is easier to carry and set up a small loom capable of weaving only narrow strips. Women weave clothing for themselves and their children on larger and heavier looms which are fixed in place in their homes in villages.

Whether wide or narrow, all strips are sewn together into pieces of cloth about the size of a blanket and are then ready to be used for clothing, carpets, or sleep coverings.

Weaving patterns vary from tribe to tribe. The king of a tribe can choose any pattern for his personal use and nobody else is allowed to wear it. Families also have distinctive patterns which they request the traveling weaver to make for them. It is considered unlucky to begin a new piece of weaving on a Friday.

A weaver in Ghana uses an easily portable small loom.
The woven patterns vary from tribe to tribe.

HOW TO MAKE A WOVEN BELT

You can weave a belt on a loom made from drinking straws.

you need

4 plastic straws

1 skein 4-ply worsted yarn

PREPARING THE LOOM

1. Cut four pieces of wool, each 80″ (2 m) long.

2. Cut ½″ (1 cm) off the end of a straw and slide it to the middle of one of the pieces of yarn.

3. Then pull both ends of the yarn through the long straw. Sucking them through helps.

4. Thread the other three straws exactly the same way.

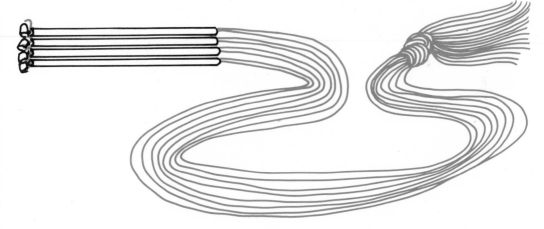

5. Tie the ends of the yarn together into a loose knot.

WEAVING

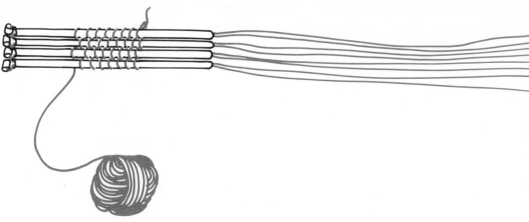

6. Knot the end of the wool on the skein to one straw.
Then weave the wool in and out.

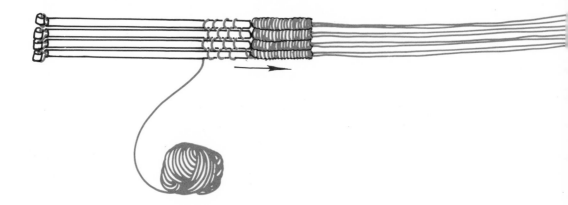

7. When you have done about 3″ to 4″ (7 to 10 cm), push the weaving down off the straws.
Continue weaving and pushing the work off the straws until the belt is long enough to go almost around your waist.

FINISHING

8. Pull off the four straws. Undo the loose knot you made at the beginning.

MAKING THE TIES

9. Tie the ends into a tight knot.
Let 8″ (20 cm) -long ends hang and cut off any extra.

WHAT ELSE YOU CAN DO

The directions given are for a belt up to 32″ (80 cm) -waist measurement. Cut wool longer for larger waist sizes.

Other ways to finish the belt: braid the yarn ends or sew on snappers to fit your waist.

Use variegated wool yarn for a belt of many colors.

You can make a group project. Sew many strips together and donate the finished blanket to a local charity.

If you do not want to weave strips, you can sew ribbons together.

Or you can cut colored paper into 2″ (5 cm) -wide strips. First cut a piece of wrapping paper into the size of wall hanging you want to make. Then glue on the cut paper strips in a patchwork pattern. This is nice for a gift.

If you want to know more about weaving and how it is done on a loom, try to find a weaver in your community and look for books on the subject.

Bambulina

A *bambulina* is a bright-colored weaving from South America. Say the word *bambulina* out loud and it bubbles around your mouth just like the little pompons that decorate it. The instructions show how to make a *bambulina* using a piece of burlap or other loosely woven material, and how to unweave it by pulling threads out to give it the lacy look.

A *bambulina* weaving from Colombia called the Tree of Life, which can be used as a Christmas door decoration.

HOW TO MAKE A BAMBULINA

you need

½ yard (½ m) burlap
½ yard (½ m) ball fringe in three different colors
A few yards of knitting wool or heavy thread
Sewing necessaries

UNWEAVING THE FABRIC

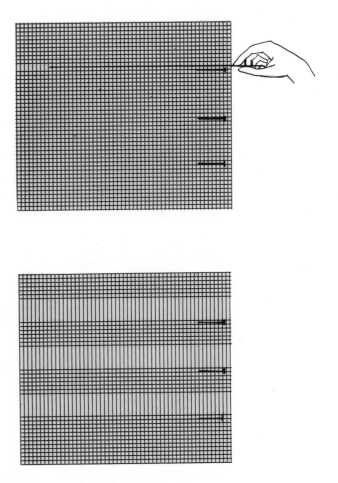

1. Cut a piece of burlap 18"×18" (45×45 cm). Cut off the selvage.

2. Divide the fabric into four equal spaces and mark with three pins.

3. Above the pin, grasp the end of a thread at one edge and pull it out.

4. Keep pulling out threads one at a time until the space above the pin is 2" (5 cm). Repeat this procedure above the other two pins.

MAKING THE DIAMOND SPACES

5. Cut 4″ (10 cm) lengths of yarn. Use them to tie a bunch of burlap threads together with a double knot and cut off the extra yarn. Continue tying the burlap all across the fabric in the three spaces. Each bunch of threads should be about 1″ (2 cm) wide.

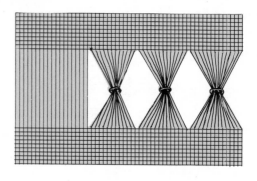

This completes the basic weaving, which can be turned into a wall hanging or a vest to wear.

A WALL HANGING

1. Hem all four edges by turning the fabric under about ½″ (1 cm) and topstitch by machine or by hand.

2. Sew a ½″ (1 cm) pleat at the top of the fabric.

3. Sew ½″ (1 cm) pleats between the diamond rows.

4. Slide ¼″ (5 mm) dowel sticks into all the pleats.

5. Sew on rows of ball fringe.

6. Make a hanger from the wool yarn and attach it to the top of the *bambulina*.

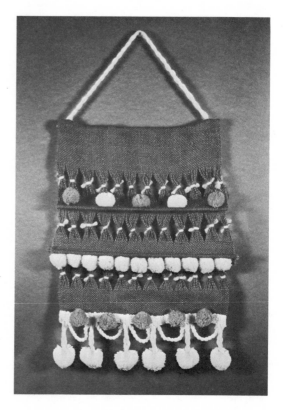

A VEST

Cut the burlap according to a paper pattern. Before sewing up the seams, mark carefully where you want the unwoven strips. Then pull threads and continue with the instructions. Do NOT make any pleats as dowel sticks are not needed.

WHAT ELSE YOU CAN DO

Balancing Acrobat

The balancing toy is a favorite in many countries. The figure, which may be an acrobat, a clown, or an animal, can be held quite still or twirled on its stand. You and your friends can have a running race, balancing it on your finger tips. The person running the longest or the fastest is the winner.

The abstract figure represents the monkey god (from India).

HOW TO MAKE A BALANCING TOY

The toy can be made with many different things, and you can choose from the list whatever you find around the house. The material that is easiest to use is listed first.

you need

FOR THE BODY:

A cork, or

A piece of wood, or

A block of styrofoam, bought in the store or cut from packing foam (electric knife is best)

FOR THE ARMS:

2 pieces of thin dowel stick, about 7″ (18 cm) long, or

2 new pencils, sharpened

FOR THE BALANCES:

Clay rolled into 2 balls, or

2 pieces of wood, or

2 sewing spools, or

2 beads

FOR THE PIVOT:

A long sewing needle, or

A long nail, or

A toothpick

1. Assemble the parts as shown in the illustration. *Note the angle at which the arms are stuck into the body (less than a right angle).* Use any glue or tool that is helpful.

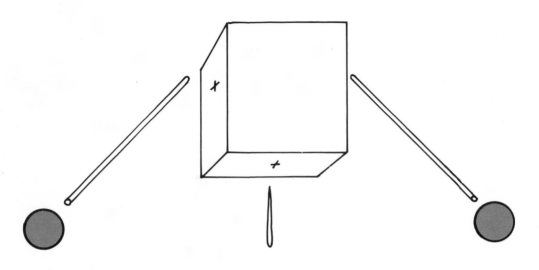

2. Balance the toy on the tip of your finger. Most toys will balance right away, but perhaps not evenly. Move the pivot or adjust the balance by adding or taking away bits of clay.

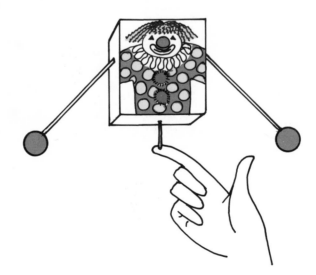

WHAT ELSE YOU CAN DO

Decorate the toy to look like a clown, a tightrope walker, a dancer, or an athlete, or paste on a photo of yourself.

It is not necessary to balance the toy exactly, but some people spend hours adjusting it perfectly.

The toy can be balanced on your finger or a table, or you can make a special stand for it from a piece of wood or a box.

You can cut the body into an animal or any other shape.
You can make this toy much larger.

Matryoshka Disappearing Toy

A favorite toy of Russian children is a *matryoshka* set of different-size dolls. Each hollow wooden doll is a little bit bigger than the next one and fits neatly over it. Most sets have five or six dolls, but a wood carver once made a set of fifty-six.

Matryoshka means grandmother, and the toy received its name because grandmothers entertain their grandchildren with the dolls when they baby-sit, and the dolls are decorated with the babushka head scarf popular with grandmothers. In the old days grandfather carved the dolls by hand, but now they are made on a lathe. You can have the fun of a nesting toy by making boxes in different sizes from paper or thin cardboard.

HOW TO MAKE THE DISAPPEARING TOY

The instructions show how to make a box on which you paint a *matryoshka* doll. Make five or more boxes in different sizes so that they fit into each other and one doll after another disappears.

you need

8″ (20 cm) paper square
Scissors

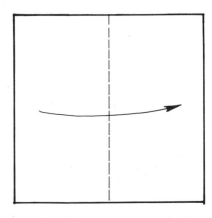

1. Fold the square in half.

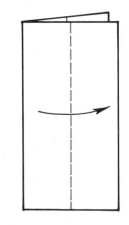

2. Fold in half again. UN-FOLD.

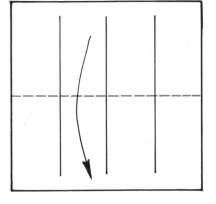

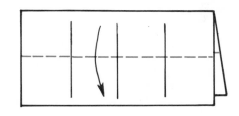

3. Fold it in half and in half again the other way. UNFOLD.

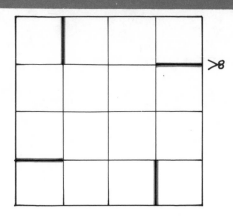

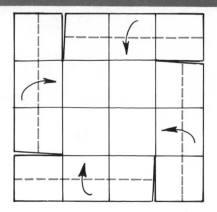

4. Cut in one small square exactly as shown, in four places.

5. Double the edges of the paper by creasing on the dotted lines.

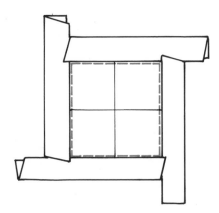

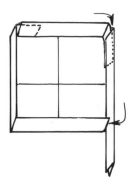

6. Stand the four doubled edges upright.

7. Bend the piece that sticks out to the inside of the box and tuck it under the next edge—you have to open the paper a bit. Repeat this on the other three corners. It seems harder to do than it actually is.

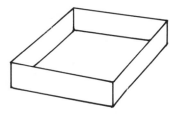

8. Crease all corners and edges sharply.

9. *The box lid* is made exactly the same, using an 8¼″ (20.5 cm) paper square.

WHAT ELSE YOU CAN DO

Make a nest of five boxes using paper squares 4", 5", 6", 7", and 8" (10, 12.5, 15, 17.5, and 20 cm).

For the lids, cut five squares just a little larger. You can draw *matryoshka* dolls on the boxes.

Use typing paper, gift wrap, shelf paper, or thin cardboard.

The illustrations show boxes from different countries, and you can decorate your paper boxes to look like them.

Use crayon, paint, embroidery, paste-ons, cutouts, sequins, used stamps, and felt-tip pens.

Finish the boxes with a THIN coating of white glue to protect them.

Make a large treasure chest.

Use boxes as building blocks.

Turn a box into a basket by adding a paper strip handle.

Wrap a gift in nested boxes.

Karagos Puppet

In remote Greek villages everyone looks forward for months to the visit of the traveling puppet theater. Posters appear in local shop windows announcing the arrival of Karagos, the wild and funny hero of the show. On the announced date a cloth screen is set up in the corner of the local cafe. Nobody misses a performance, whether the troupe is there one night or more. Each evening a different play is given and the main actor is always Karagos, meaning "Dark Eye." He may be disguised as a policeman, detective, spy, cook, businessman, soldier, magician, or in women's clothes, but whatever his role, the audience always recognizes him by his large hooked nose and humped back.

Karagos is poor and uneducated, but he is smart. Through hard work and cool cunning he catches thieves and murderers, wins out over rich

A Karagos sheet from Greece. There are different sheets for forty-four standard stories. Each sheet illustrates the characters involved in one tale.

landlords, and sees through cover-ups. He is always clowning around, making fun of the mayor and politicians. His best friend, Hachivat, helps him chase criminals or rescue a girl in trouble, and they get into plenty of fights.

All the characters are shadow puppets made from leather that has been treated with oil to make it transparent. The clothes are painted in bright colors, which show up when the light shines through them.

Karagos came to Greece from Turkey, but he is not so popular there now, except for children's birthday parties, when a puppet group may be hired to perform. In England the most famous puppets are called Punch and Judy. In Italy Punch is called Pulcinella, and in Austria and Germany he is known as Kasperle.

HOW TO MAKE A KARAGOS ·PUPPET

you need

Thin cardboard (manila file folders)

Tracing paper

¼″ (5 mm) -thick dowel stick

2 double-pronged brads

Crayons or paints

1. On the tracing paper, trace the outline of the three full-size pieces shown.

2. Place the tracing paper on the cardboard and cut out Karagos.

3. Color Karagos.

4. Connect the pieces with the brads.

hole for stick

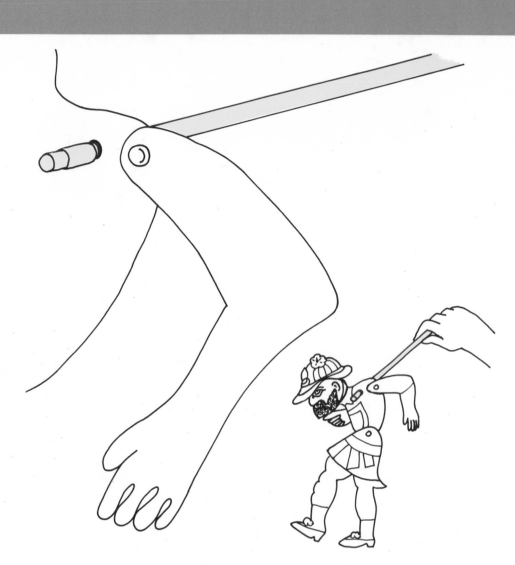

5. Pierce a hole through the circle at the shoulder. Cut stick 15″ (35 cm) long and slide it through the shoulder hole. Wind two pieces of sticky tape on the stick, in front of the puppet to act as a stopper.

HINTS:

If you do not have brads, you can hold the puppet together with yarn knotted on both sides of the paper.

To make puppets transparent, color them first; then brush them with any oil (salad, baby, linseed). Dry them with paper towels. Cover them with any clear varnish or craft finish.

HOW TO MOVE KARAGOS

Move the stick up and down; doesn't he look as though he is jumping?

Move the stick sideways; isn't he rushing to an emergency?

Make him turn a somersault.

Attach another stick to his elbow. This gives greater flexibility. Practice moving and twirling both sticks.

WHAT ELSE YOU CAN DO

Present a puppet play in a dark room. Use a white sheet or a piece of tissue paper as a screen. Place a lamp or flashlight at the back. Throw shadows by holding the puppets between the light and the screen.

Write a story about Karagos and his friend Hachivat, or make up a story about school, or invent a detective story or monster tale. Then make puppets for the characters in your story.

Rehearse the play with a friend several times. Then invite your family and friends to see the play. Let the puppets tell jokes and talk with the audience. Ask them questions.

Find out about puppet theater in other countries.

Make small holes all over the paper puppets with a needle. This is called pinpricking. Beautiful patterns will show when you shine the light through the puppet. Indonesian puppets are decorated in this way.

Lucky Hand Charm

The sign of the hand has been a protective symbol since the day of the caveman and appears in different forms in many societies. The Bible tells of the Prophets laying on hands to bless or heal. In the Middle East the lucky hand is a popular charm often worn by children on a thin chain around their neck to ward off the glance of a person who may wish them ill.

In Iran the hand is called the Hand of Fatima or simply *dast*, the hand. Fatima was the daughter of Mohammed the founder of the Moslem religion. To the Shi'ite sect in Iran the five fingers represent the five most important Moslem figures: Mohammed, Ali, Hussein, Fatima, and Hasan. The hand is always abstract in accordance with the tradition laid down by the sacred book, the Koran, which forbids making realistic pictures of people and animals. All craft objects are decorated with geometric shapes and graceful curves. The lucky hand often appears on walls of religious buildings and can be found on fountains, domes of mosques, and tombs. It is a popular piece of jewelry, either very plain or inlaid with valuable gems.

The instructions show how to make an outline design from wire. Silver wire is normally used for jewelry of this kind and can be found in most craft stores. Wire from the hardware store is suitable, if you can bend it easily with a pair of pliers. Copper wire is preferable. Sixteen-gauge thickness is comfortable to work with, yet will hold its shape.

FIGURE AND HAND. This sculpture by Iranian artist Parviz Tanavoli, is based on the traditional Tazia Tower of the Hand of Fatima, which is carried in parades. It is made from copper and brass on a wood base 101″ (252 cm) high.

HOW TO MAKE A WIRE PENDANT

you need

25″ (60 cm) wire

A pair of pliers; long-nosed kind is best

Bend the wire into the shape of the hand shown here. Cut off any extra wire. If the ends are scratchy, smooth them with steel wool, sandpaper, or a fine file.

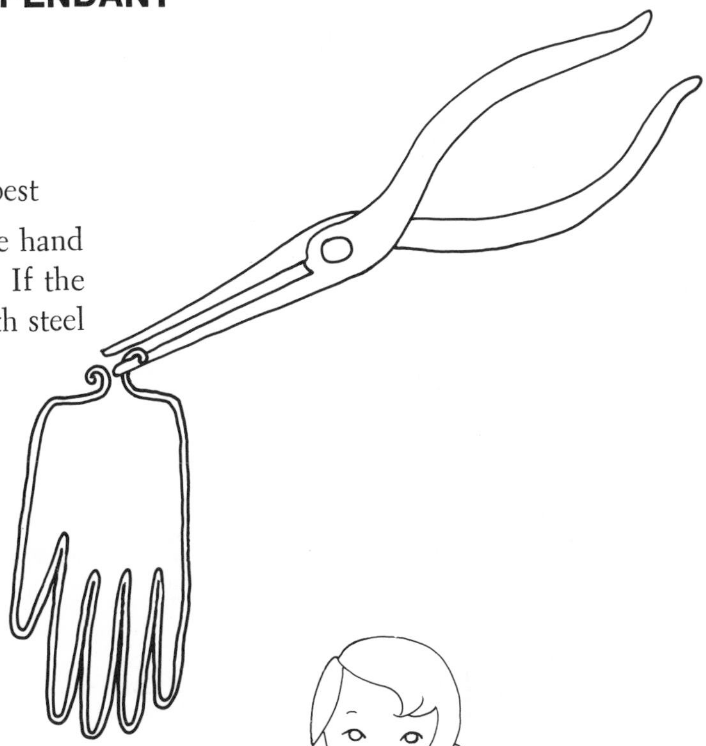

WHAT ELSE YOU CAN DO

Hang the pendant from velvet ribbon or a long shoelace.

Use the charm on a bracelet.

Make your own design of a hand, perhaps with fingers wide apart.

Paint wire with acrylic paint.

Hang beads from the ends of the fingers. This is a traditional decoration in the Middle East. To increase the power of the hand amulet, other symbols may be attached to it: fish, ox head, frog, reptile.

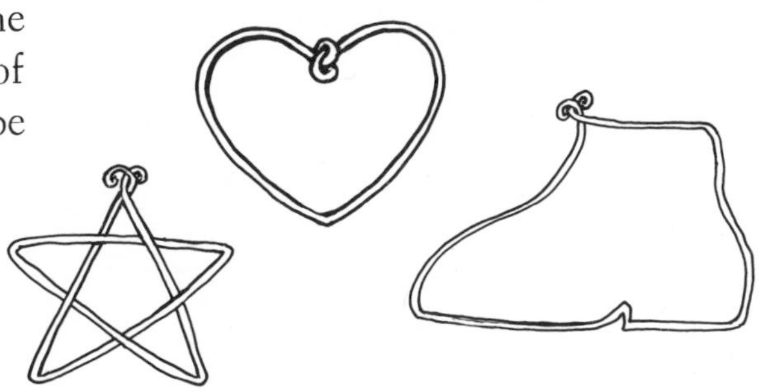

Fantastic Sculptures

Many empty oil drums are available for recycling in the Caribbean island country of Haiti. Some of them are converted into musical drums by players in native steel bands, but Georges Liautaud had other ideas. He transformed the drums into fantastic sculptures of animals, mermaids, devils, saints, and voodoo spirits. Voodoo is the religious cult which was widely practiced in Haiti. Its supernatural world is reflected in Liautaud's sculptures.

His method is to cut off the top and bottom of a steel drum and cut open the side, leaving a flat sheet 6′ by 3′ (2 m by 1 m). He scratched on his drawing and cut it out with heavy shears. Cutout slits and circles added

Metal Sculpture by Georges Liautaud

an airy look. After he had made a few sculptures, he found it easier to draw a paper pattern first, which allowed him to make changes without ruining a whole steel sheet. He continually improved his technique, chiseling and hammering in eyes, ears, and other features and smoothing over any rough parts with files and sandpaper. When he was completely pleased with the look of the sculpture he etched in his name.

Liautaud was interested in mechanics even as a child and always enjoyed working with tools. He became a blacksmith and eventually, as a sideline, he hammered simple iron crosses to be placed on graves. Adding curlicues led to the sculptures, many of which are now prized in art museums. He innovated an entirely new art form and inspired other Haitians to make steel drum sculptures.

You can make similar metal sculptures from thin aluminum, which is sold by the sheet in art stores. You can substitute aluminum pie plates, broiler pans, and similar disposable containers, cutting off the rims first. The only drawback is that your sculpture will be quite small. The material that looks and handles most like steel drums is aluminum flashing, which is sold in hardware stores for fixing roofs. It can be cut with tin snips or an old pair of strong scissors (good scissors will be ruined), and designs can be hammered in.

Sculpture cut out from a steel drum by Haitian artist Seresier Louisjuste. It is mounted on a wood board covered with orange burlap.

HOW TO MAKE A FISH

you need

Aluminum-foil sheeting (from an art store), or

Aluminum flashing (from a hardware store)

Pencil

An old pair of scissors or tin snips

Hammer, nail, screw driver

Fine sandpaper

Thick pile of newspapers to work on

Note: Flashing comes rolled and has to be flattened. Cut a piece as large as you need for the fish. Then place it between two piles of newspapers or two magazines. Slide the hammer across, pressing down heavily. Without the protection of the newspaper, the flashing will have hammer marks.

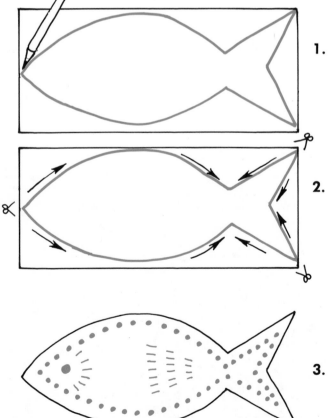

1. Draw the outline of the fish on the aluminum. Redraw it until you are satisfied.

2. Cut it out. Always cut INTO corners, as shown by the direction of the arrows.

3. Draw on circles and short lines.

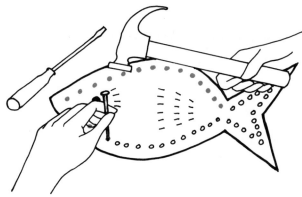

4. Hammer them in with the nail and the screw driver.

5. Smooth any rough edges by sliding the hammer head across them. Sandpaper if necessary.

WHAT ELSE YOU CAN DO

Make birds, bats, comic-book characters, acrobats, iguanas, voodoo spirits, robots, flowers, trees, a windmill, Tolkien people, whatever you can think of and make them as weird as possible.

The basic directions shown for the fish produce a raised design with perhaps a few holes going all the way through the aluminum. You can enlarge nail holes by inserting the scissor tips and twirling them around GENTLY.

Try making patterns by hammering washers, screw heads, ball-point pens, the ends of dowel sticks, and other objects.

Make small and large holes.

Punch the flashing from both sides for raised and indented patterns.
Snip and curl the edges.

Crimp the edges with a pair of long-nosed pliers, bending first to the right and then to the left. First try it out on a piece of scrap.

Nail the sculpture on a painted wooden board in such a way that the nails are part of the design.

Hang several cutouts from a wire clothes hanger as a mobile.
Make a belt buckle or Christmas tree ornaments.

Sandpainting

According to the lore of the Navaho Indians of the southwestern United States, the gods taught medicine men to make pictures in the sand. The pictures cure illness or lift a curse and must be made and destroyed in one day or one night, otherwise they will bring bad luck.

All members of a tribe meet in the large medicine lodge. A base layer of natural desert sand is spread on the floor, about one to three inches thick, and the sick person is seated in the middle. The medicine man and his trainees make the sacred design with colored sands by letting them trickle between their fingers as they slowly move their hands. Tribe members sing and pray for the help of the Great Spirit. The sand paintings illustrate Indian legends about male and female gods, about the spirits of the mountains, thunder and lightning, animals, and plants, whose help is needed to cure the patient.

The sizes of the pictures vary from three to thirty-five feet, and it takes at least three years of practice to be able to make the straight lines and perfect circles freehand. Sometimes a tightly stretched piece of string is used as a guide for a long line. The colors have the following meanings:

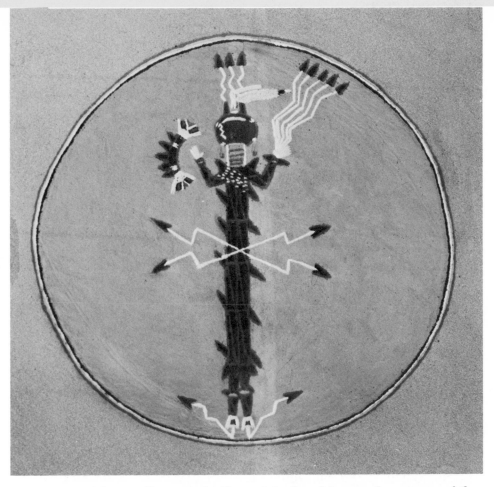

Monster Slayer on the Face of the Sun. Monster slayer is one of the two warrior twins, children of the sun. He gave horses to the Navaho Indians. He is wearing obsidian armor and carries lightning arrows in one hand and a thunder bolt in the other. He stands on lightning arrows. The circle represents the sun and is usually blue.

white for east, black for north, blue for south, yellow for west, and red for sunshine. The colors are ground from natural materials. Limestone is used for white, wood and charcoal for black, sandstone for red and brown.

Certain tribes believe sand paintings should be kept secret, but recently some Indian artists have shared them with the outside world. Instead of making loose sand pictures on the ground, they apply sand mixed with dry glue grains on a board. The picture is left outside at night and the morning dew moistens the glue. The sun bakes the picture and binds the sand permanently to the board.

HOW TO MAKE SAND PAINTINGS

You can buy white or colored sand or you can get it from a sand pit, on a beach, or in the desert. Most kinds of sand can be dyed, but some construction sand will not take color.

Use strong dye colors such as black, brown, scarlet, royal blue, kelly green, tangerine, aqua, and yellow.

COLORING THE SAND

you need for each color

1 tablespoon liquid fabric dye (Rit or Tintex), or
1 teaspoon powder dye
½ cup sifted sand
¾ cup hot tap water
A plastic cup or container

Mix the dye with the hot water. Add the sand.
Let soak for at least two hours.
Sand will be at the bottom of the cup.
Slowly pour off the colored water.
Dry the sand by spreading it on newspaper or paper towels.
After it is dried, pour the sand into a cup or paper plate.

MAKING THE PAINTING

you need

A piece of cardboard
Felt-tip pen
White glue
Clear shellac or varnish or craft finish (optional)

1. Draw the design on the cardboard with felt-tip pen.

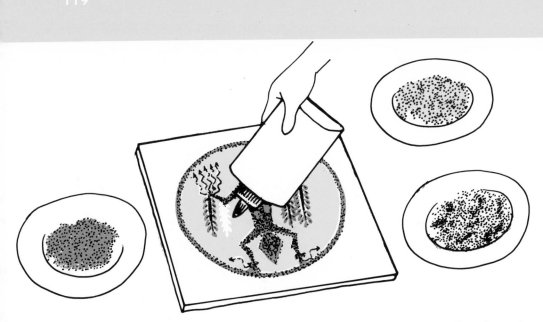

2. Cover small areas of one color with glue. Drop the colored sand on it. Let it dry for a few minutes.

Tilt the painting and let any loose sand drop onto a piece of newspaper so that it is easy to run the extra sand back into the paper cup.

3. Continue gluing and sanding parts of the picture until it is complete.

4. When the painting is dry, coat it with clear shellac, varnish, or craft finish.

Tin Lantern

A pierced-tin lantern was the usual way of lighting about two hundred years ago. It protected the candle inside from being blown out by the wind and prevented fires.

Handmade lanterns are still produced in Spain, often in a workshop that is part of a home. The whole family helps. Even very small children perform simple tasks, such as attaching handles. As they get older they cut and hammer the tin sheets. Soldering the parts together is left to the father.

The completed lanterns are shipped all over the world for indoor and outdoor decorations.

HOW TO MAKE A TIN LANTERN

you need

A large empty tin can
A short candle
Hammer
Nails of different sizes
Wire for hanging

PREPARING THE CAN

The can first has to be filled with a resistant material, otherwise it will bend out of shape when you hammer holes into it. Fill the can with shredded newspaper or with ice.

SHREDDED NEWSPAPER METHOD

Hammer two holes about 1″ (3 cm) away from the bottom of the can to let out extra water later on. Fill the can with newspaper shredded into small pieces. Wet the paper as you stuff the can and pound it until it is almost as hard as a rock. Hold it in with sticky tape across the top.

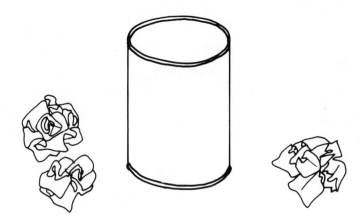

ICE METHOD

Fill the can with water and freeze it in the freezer compartment of the refrigerator for one or two days; or freeze it outside in the wintertime. If some of the ice melts during hammering put it back for refreezing.

HAMMERING A PIERCED LANTERN

1. Draw a dot design on the can with a felt-tip pen or crayon.

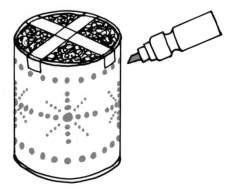

2. Hammer in the holes. Put the can on folded towels to absorb water.

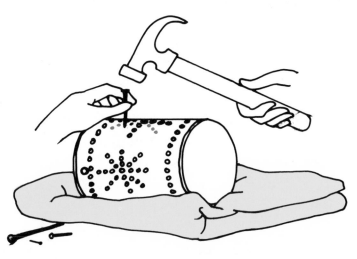

3. Hammer two holes near the top for a hanging wire.

4. Remove the paper or ice. If the bottom of the frozen can is buckled, hammer it in.

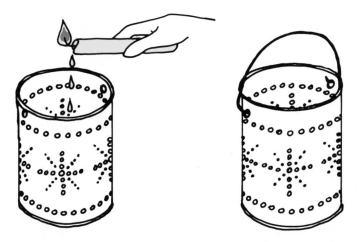

5. Glue the candle into the lantern like this: Light the candle and drip some wax into the floor of the lantern, blow it out quickly and put the candle in the soft wax. Keep your eye on the flame all the time, so you don't burn yourself.

Make lanterns from small tin cans and use them as table decorations. If you make one for every guest, they can take them home.

Bookbinding

Centuries ago, when books were rare and therefore very valuable, they were covered with beautiful handmade bindings. The craftsmen in Florence, Italy, were famous for their gold-tooled leatherwork and they still continue this tradition by producing fine handmade leather and paper bindings. Expert binding of a book takes thirty-six separate hand processes. It is claimed that the most expensive bookbinding in the world was made by an English craftsman at a cost of £15,000 (approximately $37,500). The binding had an inlay of solid gold studded with precious stones.

Bookbinding in the Florentine way is a precise craft, requiring special equipment. But there is a type of book covering that is much easier to do. It is called *remboitage*, which means "to enclose an old book in new covers." You can bind books in this simple way, using paper with traditional Florentine or other designs. For a first project, bind one of your favorite paperback books. All you need is a sheet of gift-wrap paper and white glue. Later you can turn inexpensive scrapbooks, note pads, or address books into good-looking birthday or Christmas gifts.

The leather-bound book decorated with gold leaf was made in 1920 by an Italian bookbinder, Cecchi. The paperback book is bound with a sunburst patterned paper according to the directions. The spine and corners are reinforced with red paper.

HOW TO BIND A BOOK

you need

Paperback book you want to cover
Cardboard
Gift-wrap paper
White glue

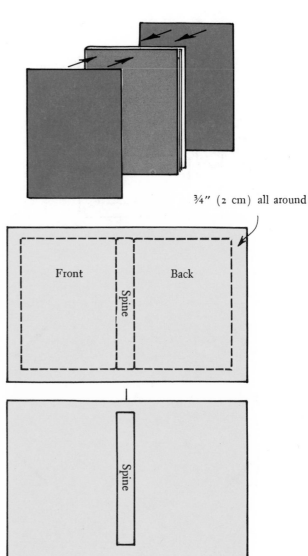

¾″ (2 cm) all around

1. Cut two pieces of cardboard the exact size of the book. Glue them to the front and the back of the book. Put it under a stack of heavy books for fifteen minutes.

Front   Spine   Back

Spine

2. Cut the gift wrap the size of the front, the spine, and the back of the book and add ¾″ (2 cm) all around the four edges.

3. Mark the center of the paper and place the spine of the book on the wrong side of the paper. Draw a pencil line around the spine.

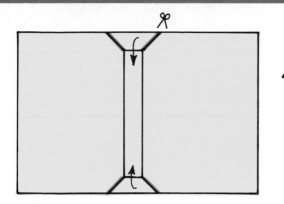

4. Cut the top and bottom of the paper as shown. Fold the shaded pieces on the dotted line and glue them down.

5. Cover the back of the spine with glue and press the gift wrap against it until the glue is dry.

6. Glue the gift wrap to the front and the back of the closed book.

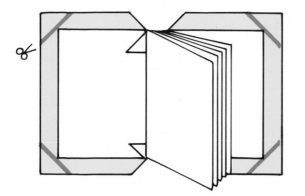

7. Open the book and cut the four corners as shown.

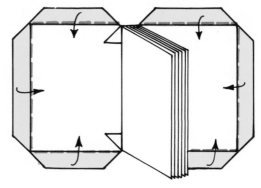

8. Fold the edges over and glue them to the inside of the book.

END PAPERS

End papers, which are glued to the inside of the cover, are usually made from plain colored paper to blend with the binding.

9. Cut 2 pieces of paper the same size as the book. Cut ½″ (1 cm) off the top and ¼″ (½ cm) off the long side.

10. Glue the papers flush against the inside covers of the book, leaving ¼″ (½ cm) exposed on the three outside edges.

WHAT ELSE YOU CAN DO

Turn inexpensive notebooks, diaries, and address books into expensive-looking gifts.

For a vacation diary, paste cutouts from postcards and leaflets to the cardboard to be used for the binding.

Any paper binding can be reinforced by wiping craft glue or Mod-Podge over it. This also gives a shiny finish.

Use fabric or self-stick plastic (Con-Tact®, Marvalon) to bind your books.

Easter Egg Cracking

Every year around Easter, Swiss boys and girls carrying Easter eggs meet in the town square of Zurich. They are ready for the competition to find who has the hardest egg—the one capable of denting everyone else's. Before the great day, contestants shop for eggs with the most pointed ends and hard-boil them. They leave some plain, but color or decorate others.

In the photo you can see a girl holding her egg, waiting for the other girl to try and crack it. After her try, the opposite ends of the eggs are held up and the other girl has her turn. A contestant wins the opponent's egg as soon as he has dented both ends.

Another game of egg cracking is played by young people who try to dent each other's eggs with coins. This is called *eiertutschen*. One player throws a coin from a certain distance, attempting to break the other's egg. If the coin does not stick in the egg, he loses the money. If the coin sticks in the egg, the coin thrower wins the egg.

Some players engage in swapping eggs and become quite expert at selecting "good eggs"—those that are harder and more pointed.

All over the Christian world Easter is the season for games with eggs. Decorated eggs are exchanged as gifts. They may be dyed in one color, or a family may spend hours together painting Ukrainian *pysanky* eggs.

The costliest eggs ever made were commissioned by Czar Alexander III of Russia to give to his wife at Easter. Every year the court jeweler, Fabergé, created a new egg which had to contain a surprise. One year a rooster popped out of the egg every hour, spread its wings, and returned inside the shell. Another egg, when opened, revealed a replica of the imperial coach, made of gold and precious jewels.

Each year the court would wonder what marvel Fabergé would come up with next year.

Many people like to decorate eggs in the style of Fabergé, using blown egg shells, gold paper, colored beads, and rickrack.

At Easter life revives after a long winter, and the egg as a fertility symbol dates back to before the Christian era. Although the eggs we eat are laid by chickens, why are Easter eggs brought by the bunny? Because the hare breeds quickly and produces large litters; and it is always amazing to see a chick start its life by breaking through the shell. In time these two symbols merged in the story of the Easter bunny.

HOW TO DECORATE EGGS

Another Swiss custom is decorating eggs with nature's herbs and leaves. Onion skins dye the eggs a rich brown color, except the area that is covered by a fresh green leaf and, therefore, remains white.

you need

White eggs
Small leaves or herbs, such as parsley
Cast-off nylon stocking or panty hose, or small
mesh gauze, or bandage
Brown outer leaves of 3 onions (enough for 6 eggs)

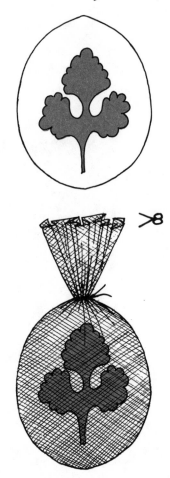

1. Wet the leaves and arrange them on an egg.

2. Cover the egg with a piece of nylon and tie the end with thread or string. Cut it off about 1″ (2 cm) away from the egg.

3. Place several eggs in a pot with the brown onion skins, and cover with water.

4. Bring to a boil and then simmer on low heat for 20 minutes.

5. Remove leaves and nylon. Run cold water over the eggs.

WHAT ELSE YOU CAN DO

Color the eggs with food dyes instead of onion skins.

Like many Swiss families, have an early morning Easter egg hunt at home. When all the eggs have been found, use them in an egg-cracking contest. Protect your egg by covering most of it with your hand and exposing just the tip. The person who has the last uncracked egg is the winner and gets a prize.

Oware Game

Supposing you bought a raffle ticket and won a trip to Africa. You could travel from one country to another, making friends with young people who live there. After visiting two or three countries you say to yourself, "Hey, I know how to play their favorite game. Everywhere I go they play with seeds on a wooden board. It's fun and when I get home I'll play it with my friends." The name of the game varies depending on the region. *Oware* and *mankala* are two names that mean "transferring."

In the West African country of Mali the game is called the Game of the Universe or Star Play. The seeds represent stars. Six cups are on the side of man and six cups are on the side of woman. The end cups are East and West.

Most often the game is played around noon, when it is hot and best to sit quietly. If you play *oware* in the morning, you are considered lazy; but it is bad luck to play at night.

The picture shows a wooden *oware* board with carved decorations. Make your own game board from wood or clay and paint on designs about sports and hobbies you like.

HOW TO MAKE AN OWARE GAME BOARD

you need

2 empty egg cartons
sticky tape

1. Cut off and throw away the lids.

2. Cut off two egg cups from one carton. Attach one to each end of the other carton with sticky tape, as shown.

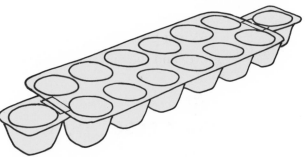

MARKERS

You need 48 seeds, which can be dried beans, peanuts, small pebbles or marbles, or small pieces of cardboard.

PREPARATION

Place the board between two players.

Each player owns the six cups on his side and the end cup on his right, which is for storing the seeds he wins.

Put four seeds in each of the twelve playing cups.

PLAYING

Always play counterclockwise (go in a circle to your left). The first player, let's call her Akua, picks up four seeds from any one of the cups on her left. The other player, let's call him Kwame, does the same thing, taking the seeds out of one of his cups and spreading them one at a time in the cups to his left. They keep taking turns, always taking out all the seeds in the cup. The number of seeds in the cups keeps changing.

WINNING

When Kwame drops the *last* seed in one of Akua's cups and there are already two or three seeds in it, he wins all the seeds in that cup. He stores them in the end cup on his right. Akua stores the seeds she wins in her cup.

When there are no more seeds left in any of the twelve cups, the game is over and the player with the most seeds wins.

WHAT ELSE YOU CAN DO

As there are so many different rules for *oware*, you can invent your own rules. How about starting with three or five seeds in each cup? How about a rule that you can only win if there are three seeds in two cups next to each other? You can change the rules to make the game easy or difficult.

To make the highest score, plan your moves ahead.

Play the game with three or four players.

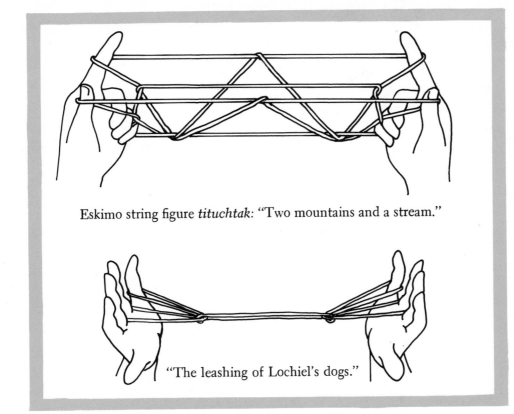

Eskimo string figure *tituchtak:* "Two mountains and a stream."

"The leashing of Lochiel's dogs."

String Magic Trick

If you have ever twiddled a piece of string, you know it can fascinate you for quite a while. People all over the world have made up string games using manufactured string, plant fibers, and even reindeer sinews.

String games are most popular with American Indians and Pacific Islanders. Best known is "cat's cradle," but this is only one of many string figures. It probably originated in Asia and spread to Europe.

Some figures are found in many countries, but others are found in only one location. "The leashing of Lochiel's dogs" which is played in Scotland, is called "crow's feet" by the Eskimos. String games are sometimes thought to be magical. Before the months-long winter night sets in, Eskimos try to catch the sun in string meshes to prevent it from disappearing to the south.

Most string games are played by two people who take turns in lifting off the loops of string from each other's hands. One person can play alone by using a larger loop of string around the knees or using the mouth.

HOW TO PERFORM A STRING TRICK

For this trick, hang a ring on a piece of string which is then stretched between another person's two thumbs.
The challenge is to remove the ring without taking the string off the thumbs.

you need

A piece of string about 24″ (60 cm) long
A ring

1. Knot the ends of the string together. Hang the ring on the string. Ask another person to hold the string looped on their two outstretched thumbs.

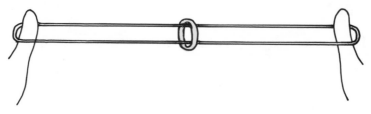

2. With your left hand grasp the upper string, pull it forward and down. Keep holding it.

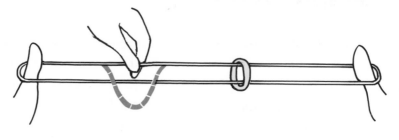

3. With your right hand grasp the other string from UNDERNEATH. Pull it in front of the other string and then loop it over the other person's thumb.

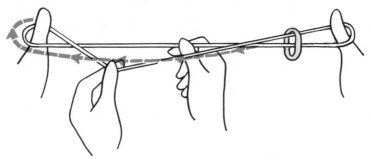

4. With your right hand grasp the upper string on the right of the ring and loop it over the other person's thumb on your left.

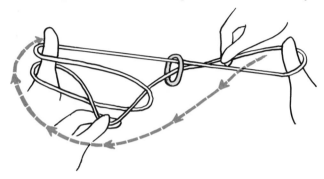

5. Let go of the piece of string which is still held in your left hand. The ring drops off while the string is still looped on the other person's thumbs.

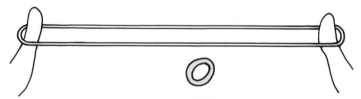

Practice this trick a few times with someone in your family. If the ring does not fall off, check step 4 and make sure that you have placed the loop on the thumb exactly as shown. If you have twisted the string first, it will not work. After a few times you will be able to do it automatically. Carry a piece of string with you and you can amaze people on a bus or when you are waiting somewhere.

These words may help you remember the trick:

FORWARD AND DOWN.
FROM UNDERNEATH: DOWN AND LOOP.
LOOP OVER THUMB.

WHAT ELSE YOU CAN DO

You can use a bracelet or other circular object instead of a ring.

With a friend, loop a piece of string back and forth from his hands onto your hands. Invent your own string patterns.

Information about materials required for making the craft projects is usually given in the text. Most are obtainable in supermarkets, dime, and department stores. For local craft stores, see the Yellow Pages of your phone book under "Arts and Crafts Supplies."

The following additional information may be helpful:

ACRYLIC PAINTS

Sold in art and craft stores. They are easy to use and can be thinned with water. Paint brushes can be washed out with water, but it must be done as soon as you have finished painting or the paint will harden and make the brush useless for future use.

CLAY

Self-hardening clay is sold in powder form in art and craft stores. It keeps indefinitely until it is mixed with water. Then it can be kept in a plastic bag for a few days. It does not need to be baked or fired, but dries naturally in the air. Complete instructions are printed on the package. *Oven-baking clay* can be baked in the kitchen oven, usually for one hour at 150° and for another hour at 250°.

Both kinds of clay are available in art supply and craft stores, or write to Sculpture House Inc., 38 East 30th Street, New York, New York 10016.

DYES

The best known brands are Rit and Tintex. They are for sale in supermarkets and fabric stores. Experiment using them on different materials: fabrics, clay, sand.

LIQUID EMBROIDERY PENS

Sold in dime and fabric stores. They are useful for decorating fabrics and other materials.

SAND

Colored sand is sold in plant stores. Mason's sand, which you color yourself, is sold in builders' supply stores. Construction sand is not suitable.

WIRE

Sold in hardware stores and in the floral-supply section of dime stores.

Thank you: Folk artists everywhere, past and present.

Thank you: Craft people, friends, and strangers, authors, museums, government agencies, tourist offices, libraries, and others who have been helpful in providing information and checking many details for accuracy. I am sorry I cannot give a personal thanks to everyone.

Thank you: Pat Connolly, my editor on six books, for having faith in me.

Thank you: Anne Pellowski, Director, United Nations Children's Fund (UNICEF) Information Center, for sharing your wide knowledge.

Thank you: Henry for watching the house being turned into a temporary warehouse of folk crafts and experiments.

Thank you: Lenox Library staff for renewing loans of books endlessly.

Thank you: Barbara Davis, art teacher Lenox schools, and John Stokes, artist-in-residence, The Stockbridge School, and your students for testing the craft instructions.

Thank you: Ellen and Don Gross at Folklorica, and Kathy Shanahan and Bob Wincuinas at Out-of-Hand for loaning folk art from your stores. John and Mary Jane Bender for the loan of the Mexican *Posada* figures; Doris Bardon for the loan of the Haitian Sculpture by Louisjuste; and the Lenox Library for the loan of Dante's *Divine Comedy*.

PAGE 1 American Craft Council's Museum of Contemporary Crafts
PAGE 9 UNICEF, photo Jack Ling
PAGE 13 Bente Hamann
PAGES 15, 51, 72 (*top*), 84, 92, 94, 96, 113, 121, 124, 127 Mike Zwerling
PAGE 17 Consulate General of the Netherlands
PAGE 20 German Information Center
PAGES 25, 26 Japan National Tourist Organization
PAGE 33 Swedish Information Service
PAGES 38, 39, 40, 41 Hong Kong Tourist Association
PAGES 46, 47 Information Service, Budapest
PAGE 59 Information Department of the Consulate General of Israel
PAGES 66, 67 Information Service of India
PAGES 70, 79 (*bottom*) Embassy of Trinidad and Tobago
PAGE 71 George Tames, The New York *Times*
PAGE 72 (*bottom*) Institute of the National Museum of Zaire, Courtesy: African-American Institute
PAGE 73 (*top, center, and bottom left*) Karen Kreiss, U. S. Committee for UNICEF
PAGE 73 (*right*) Drawing of Elephant Mask based on a photograph by Maryellen Hausman, U. S. Committee for UNICEF
PAGES 75, 129 Swiss National Tourist Office
PAGE 76 Gregory Kitchen, Courtesy: Rizzoli Art Gallery
PAGE 81 The British Tourist Authority
PAGE 82 Levi, Strauss & Co.
PAGE 88 Dr. Pascal James Imperato
PAGE 100 United Nations Gift Center
PAGE 110 New York University Art Collection, Grey Art Gallery, Gift of the Ben and Abbey Grey Foundation Collection
PAGE 112 Courtesy: Selden Rodman
PAGES 116, 117 New Mexico Department of Development
PAGE 120 Spanish National Tourist Office
PAGE 131, Florence Temko
PAGE 144 Clemens Kalischer

ABOUT THE AUTHOR

FLORENCE TEMKO is the author of twelve craft books. In *Folk Crafts for World Friendship* she combines her love of crafts and travel, having visited craftspeople in twenty-eight countries. Ms Temko studied at the London School of Economics and the New School for Social Research in New York. Her audience-participating lectures and workshops have been given at many museums (including the Metropolitan Museum of Art and Cooper Union Museum) libraries, schools, and clubs. She has made two films (National Film Board of Canada and BFA Educational Films) and has appeared on many television shows in the United States and England. She was International Chairman on the executive board of the Girl Scouts of Monmouth County, New Jersey. Ms Temko introduced a course on Origami and other paper crafts at the Berkshire Community College, near Lenox, Massachusetts, where she and her husband make their home, and where she plans to establish a Paper Craft Museum.

ABOUT THE ARTIST

YAROSLAVA SURMACH MILLS is a prize-winning illustrator, who was Art Director of *Humpty Dumpty* Magazine. One of her early paintings was chosen by UNICEF for a Christmas card and for their calendar. Yaroslava's interest in folk art helped her popularize the Ukrainian custom of decorating Easter eggs in the United States. She is a graduate of Cooper Union Art School, taught at Manhattanville College and now lives in Rockland County, New York.